Blended Learning
in Action

*For all of the teachers taking risks,
failing forward, and embracing change.*

Blended Learning in Action

A Practical Guide Toward Sustainable Change

Catlin R. Tucker

Tiffany Wycoff

Jason T. Green

CORWIN

A SAGE Publishing Company

FOR INFORMATION:

Corwin
A SAGE Company
2455 Teller Road
Thousand Oaks, California 91320
(800) 233-9936
www.corwin.com

SAGE Publications Ltd.
1 Oliver's Yard
55 City Road
London EC1Y 1SP
United Kingdom

SAGE Publications India Pvt. Ltd.
B 1/I 1 Mohan Cooperative Industrial Area
Mathura Road, New Delhi 110 044
India

SAGE Publications Asia-Pacific Pte. Ltd.
3 Church Street
#10-04 Samsung Hub
Singapore 049483

Acquisitions Editor: Ariel Bartlett
Senior Associate Editor: Desirée A. Bartlett
Senior Editorial Assistant: Andrew Olson
Production Editor: Veronica Stapleton Hooper
Copy Editor: Janet Ford
Typesetter: C&M Digitals (P) Ltd.
Proofreader: Sally Jaskold
Indexer: Karen Wiley
Cover Designer: Gail Buschman
Marketing Manager: Anna Mesick

Printed in the United States of America

ISBN: 978-1-5063-4116-3

This book is printed on acid-free paper.

SFI Certified Sourcing
www.sfiprogram.org
SFI-00453

17 18 19 20 10 9 8 7 6 5 4 3

Contents

PART 4. BLENDED LEARNING: THE ROADMAP TO PERSONALIZATION

Preface

A TRAVEL GUIDE FOR THE SHARED JOURNEY

This book addresses each aspect of developing a blended learning program: from creating a blended culture and communicating with all the various stakeholders involved, to exploring classroom models and building a learning toolbox. Instead of focusing myopically on one group of stakeholders in a school community, this book was written to guide each group of stakeholders—leaders, teacher trailblazers, and teachers in a districtwide or schoolwide shift to blended learning. The journey is intended to be taken together to build appreciation for each stakeholder's perspective, and through this understanding, achieve a strong blended learning culture.

This book is broken into four parts:

Part 1: Shifting to a Blended Culture

Part 2: Blended Learning Toolbox

Part 3: Blended Learning—Exploring Classroom Models

Part 4: Blended Learning—The Roadmap to Personalization

Each part of the book is focused on supporting the entire school community in the shift to blended learning. It is equally important for leaders and classroom teachers to understand the *why* behind this shift and to appreciate the long-term benefits of shifting to a blended model. Leaders will have to manage change on a large scale and guide the shift, while individual teachers will need to learn how to employ different models and leverage technology in their classrooms in order to blend learning mediums.

Although it might be tempting for a school leader to skim Part 3, which focuses on exploring classroom models, it's important that leaders understand the models, the challenges and benefits of each, and the support teachers will need to implement different models. Leaders will also benefit from understanding what types of tools teachers will need to employ blended learning strategies. Similarly, teachers will gain insight into the larger-scale considerations of a blended learning implementation.

When all of the stakeholders in a school community understand the shifts taking place at each level, it ultimately makes school leaders and teachers more empathetic and understanding because they recognize the different challenges facing each group involved in this shift to a blended learning model. To make this connection even stronger between the leadership and teacher lenses, readers will find "Links to Leadership" sections included in the teacher-oriented chapters and "Links to the Classroom" sections included in the leader-oriented chapters. Each chapter also concludes with book study questions intended to help colleagues discuss the concepts presented in this book and apply them to their unique school settings.

Figure P.1 outlines the icons used to identify the Links to Leadership and Links to the Classroom. Additionally, the implementation strategies are organized by icons corresponding to the Blended Learning Elements of Effectiveness outlined in Chapter 3.

These icons represent the types of supports that teachers will need and the practices that align with a balanced implementation of blended learning models. The content next to each icon highlights areas and questions for teachers and leaders to consider as they shift to a blended learning model. Often these are issues that affect all teachers and may not be factors that teachers can control, so support from leaders is needed.

This book is intended to be one part of a longer conversation and journey. This journey will be shared within school teams, but it can also extend beyond individual school walls. We invite you to take part in a connected conversation about Blended Learning in Action through the hashtag #BLinAction as you read this book and transform your classroom.

FIGURE P.1 Book Icons

 Links to Leadership: Outlines considerations for school leaders in designing the blended learning program; includes strategies for supporting teachers in the successful implementation of program components.

 Links to the Classroom: Outlines considerations for teachers shifting to a blended learning model and provides support strategies teachers can employ in their classroom practice with student stakeholders.

 Building Capacity: Discusses professional development needs to support teachers in effective implementation of program components.

 Technology Utilization: Outlines specific technology needs or considerations for program components, and the redefinition of instruction through technology.

 Data Management and Usage: Provides strategy for using data as an instructional tool in the personalization of learning.

 Student Ownership: Outlines strategies for engaging students as drivers and agents of their learning.

Acknowledgments

We began our professional journey together as part of a school transformation team a little over a year ago. We are grateful to Redbird Advanced Learning for designing a professional development team representative of the different perspectives and voices in the field of blended learning. This opportunity brought the three of us together in a manner that enriched our understanding, and inspired us to share a multifaceted perspective of blended learning through the process of co-authoring this book.

We are grateful to our colleagues who helped us make the "In-Action" concept of this book a reality by sharing stories and insights from their own schools and classrooms. Rick Miller, Mike Ritzius, Kerry Gallagher, Brian Johnson, Jason Bretzmann, Kenny Bosch, Kimberly Weber, Starr Sackstein, Michael Saddler, Janet Keating, Jackie Westerfield, Dr. Polly Haldeman, and Samuel Berey lent perspectives to this work. We cannot thank you enough for the "In-Action" lenses you contributed and for the innovation you bring to your schools and the field.

We would like to also thank Kyrie Kennemore, Victoria Sandoval, Fiona Lui Martin, Conor Brown, Elaine Baez, Angel Cruz, Kristen St. Louis, Eva Oliveri, Anaya Akpalu, Paloma Velasquez, George Payne, Britney Hassett, Ian McGee, Gemma Figoni, Alyssa Girimonte, Ashley Culver, Laura Malfavon, and Dean Zweiman for providing the student perspective of learning throughout this work. Blended learning empowers students as drivers of their own learning, so we must seek to understand where they would go if only they had the keys.

To our past, present, and future students—those we will meet face-to-face in our classrooms and those we never will—we are indebted to you for the learning and inspiration you have provided and continue to provide for us throughout this shared journey.

To the children in our personal lives—Alina, Joseph, Journey, Skye, Cheyenne, and Maddox—thank you for making us always feel like students of life, ensuring we are forever learning alongside you, and thank you for your unique gifts and talents that remind us every day of the absolute necessity of more personalized learning in schools.

PUBLISHER'S ACKNOWLEDGMENTS

Corwin gratefully acknowledges the contributions of the following reviewers:

Juliette Guarino Berg
Lower School Science Specialist
The Mandell School
New York, New York

Kelly Fitzgerald
Online Learning Integration
   Specialist
Leander ISD
Leander, Texas

Freda Hicks
Principal
Perry Harrison Elementary
Pittsboro, North Carolina

Brian R. Johnson
Principal
Tilden Middle School
Philadelphia, Pennsylvania

Jessica Johnson
Elementary School Principal
District Assessment
   Coordinator
Dodgeland School District
Juneau, Wisconsin

Louis Lim
Vice-Principal
York Region District School Board
Richmond Hill, Ontario, Canada

Jacie Maslyk
Assistant Superintendent
Hopewell Area School District
Aliquippa, Pennsylvania

Theresa Stager
Principal
St. Mary Rockwood Catholic School
Rockwood, Michigan

Bonnie Tryon
MentorCoach, Past President, and
   2007 National Distinguished
   Principal
School Administrators Association
   of New York
Cobleskill, New York

Kim Weber
4th Grade Teacher
Mandell School
New York, New York

About the Authors

Catlin R. Tucker is an accomplished Google Certified Teacher, international trainer, education consultant, speaker, and author. She currently teaches in Sonoma County where she was named Teacher of the Year in 2010. She has also taught online college-level writing courses, which led to her interest in blended learning and technology integration. Catlin's first book, *Blended Learning in Grades 4–12,* is a bestseller. In 2015, Corwin published her second book, *Creatively Teach the Common Core Literacy Standards with Technology.* She authored a blended learning course for ASCD (Association for Supervision and Curriculum Development), and writes a monthly column titled "Techy Teacher" for *Educational Leadership.* Catlin earned her BA in English from UCLA and her English credential and Masters in Education from UCSB. She writes an internationally ranked education technology blog at CatlinTucker.com and is active on Twitter @Catlin_Tucker.

Tiffany Wycoff is an innovative school leader with a specialization in blended learning and school technology integration. She was an early adopter of blended learning at the K-12 level, teaching and leading in both online and face-to-face settings. Tiffany has served as a school leader at Grandview Preparatory School in Florida and The Mandell School in New York, helping both schools establish technology rich learning environments and incorporate blended learning models into the academic program. She has presented on blended learning and the use of social media in education at conferences and universities, and helped other schools transform their programs through blended learning implementation. Tiffany collaborated on the design and development of the Redbird Professional Learning Platform that provides online professional development to teachers and leaders. She holds a BA in Elementary Education and a MA in Educational Leadership from Florida Atlantic University, and an Executive MS in Technology Management from Columbia University. Tiffany writes an educational leadership blog at www.TeachOnTheEdge.com and is active on Twitter @TeachOnTheEdge.

Jason T. Green, inspired by his youth development and nonprofit work as a student at Morehouse College, has dedicated his career to creating positive change in education. As a member of the leadership team with Redbird Advanced Learning, Jason partnered with Stanford University's Graduate School of Education to re-envision professional learning. He led the design of the Redbird Professional Learning Platform that now helps prepare thousands of teachers globally for 21st century learning. Jason has traveled nationally and internationally to help schools and districts build cultures of innovation and adapt to education's changing landscape. Jason has spoken at leading universities and conferences, including Stanford, University of Pennsylvania, NCSM (National Council of Supervisors of Mathematics), and iNACOL (International Association for K–12 Online Learning), as well as being featured in the *Miami Herald,* and the *Philadelphia Inquirer* and on NBC. A Phi Beta Kappa graduate of Morehouse College, Jason is driven by the belief that all children have a right to a high-quality education. Jason holds an MBA from the Wharton School of Business and an M.S. Ed from University of Pennsylvania's Graduate School of Education. Jason has served as an adjunct professor and a board member for various nonprofits. Connect with Jason on Twitter @jasontoddgreen.

Introduction

In the three years since I wrote *Blended Learning in Grades 4–12*, technology has continued to push the conversation about what it means to be a teacher and what it means to be a learner. Schools all over the country today are rethinking the way students learn and are seeking creative new ways to weave together the best aspects of face-to-face and online learning. I've been struck by the growing interest in blended learning in recent years. *Blended Learning in Grades 4–12* has become a bestseller, which indicates that teachers and schools are hungry for concrete resources to support them in making sustainable change to improve learning.

When I first began writing about blended learning, I was making this shift alone. I did not have a school supporting me, I did not have easy access to technology, and I did not receive any formal professional development training. I was driven by the desire to make my classroom a student-centered space where my kids had the opportunity to drive their learning.

In my first book I wanted to support other teachers like me who might not have support at their school site, but wanted to rethink their approach with the goal of placing students at the center of learning. My book focused on supporting teachers with concrete strategies and resources to help them create a safe space online, encourage respectful communication online, design online tasks to engage students, and weave online work back into a student-centered classroom. I wanted to emphasize that *any* teacher could adopt a blended learning model. Even teachers with limited access to technology could get creative with just a handful of devices.

Teachers have read my book and reached out on social media to thank me for helping them to reimagine their approach to teaching. Like me, many began their journey toward a blended learning model with fear and trepidation. It's challenging to make such a radical shift in a single classroom without support from leaders or fellow teachers. This book was born out of a desire to support districts and entire schools shift from a traditional teaching model to a blended learning model.

On a trip to Puerto Rico in 2015 to train teachers on blended learning models, I had a serendipitous encounter with two other individuals, Jason Green and Tiffany Wycoff, who shared my passion for blended learning and its potential to transform learning. Jason Green, Executive Director of Blended Learning and Professional Development with Redbird Advanced Learning, has done extensive work in the field of blended learning at a schoolwide and district levels. Tiffany Wycoff is a school principal who has been both a teacher and a leader in a K-12 blended learning environment for several years.

Together we represented three different areas of expertise. Jason's focus on large scale change, Tiffany's experience as a school leader, and my work as a teacher and trainer all complemented each other and led to conversations about how we could combine our various areas of expertise to help entire districts and schools shift to blended learning. We recognize that there are various stakeholders in a school community who are responsible for making decisions if a large scale shift to a blended learning model is going to be successful.

The International Society for Technology in Education (ISTE) identifies the "Essential Conditions" needed to "effectively leverage technology for learning" and successfully implement the "ISTE Standards, tech planning and systemwide change." Among the essential conditions, ISTE emphasizes the importance of a shared vision and empowered leaders. It's crucial that a large scale change involving a shift in school culture, design, pedagogy, and technology integration begins with "a shared vision for educational technology among all education stakeholders" and that "stakeholders at every level are empowered to be leaders in effecting change."

In my last book, *Creatively Teach the Common Core Literacy Standards with Technology*, I acknowledged that "Yes, education has been disrupted. The good news is that teachers today have more tools at their disposal and more ways to connect with and learn from educators all over the world. If we can get beyond our own fear and embrace some new realities, we have an opportunity to redefine education and make learning more relevant and engaging for our students." Imagine what individual school leaders could do if they worked in partnership with teachers, parents, and students to rethink how their school approaches teaching and learning.

—*Catlin Tucker*

PART 1

Shifting to a Blended Culture

Jason T. Green

INTRODUCTION

When I attended Morehouse College in the mid-nineties, southwest Atlanta (commonly referred to as SWAT) was one of the most depressed sections of the city. Morehouse College, a prestigious historically black college steeped in a culture of excellence and a tradition of producing civic leaders, doctors, lawyers, entrepreneurs, and scientists, was situated in the heart of the SWAT. Though both the populations were predominantly African-American, the life trajectories of the students of Morehouse College and the students of the surrounding community could not have been more different.

This disparity sparked a question that would fuel my life's passion. What was special about me and my classmates that afforded us these opportunities while our counterparts lived a starkly different reality just beyond campus gates? The answer was not so difficult—education. We received a quality education early in our lives that positioned us for success. More importantly we received an education that somehow worked for each of us as individuals. But, getting to that answer was just the beginning of a much more vexing and complex problem. How do we create quality education at scale that works for every student and honors their individuality as learners?

I would go on to grapple with this question for the next 20 years. It has only been in the last few years that I see a feasible, scalable path forward. Through my work with Redbird Advanced Learning and our partnership with Stanford University, we've supported hundreds of schools in their transformation toward blended learning. When well implemented, blended learning environments create the possibility for every student to experience precisely the learning he or she needs. This is a possibility—not a guarantee.

The presence of technology alone does not imply any inherent value to teaching or learning. The other part of the equation is the intangibles, such as culture, mindset, and true preparedness of teachers and school leaders.

The technology we have today is a game changer because it can *help* create magic in the classroom—however, only to the extent that schools and teachers are prepared and engaged. Teachers can now personalize instruction and empower students in ways unthinkable before. The first section of this book is about cultivating these critical intangibles to set the stage for meaningful integration of technology in classrooms, across schools, and entire districts. It is this foundation that ultimately sets your blended learning transformation on a course for success.

CHAPTER 1

Going Blended to Meet the World

Learning should look like it is built for each student, it should be unique to them, not just the same thing for every single student. If it looks designed for the student you can draw their attention and keep it.

—Kyrie Kennemore, 9th Grade

SCALING BLENDED LEARNING TRANSFORMATION

We've written this book with systemwide transformation in mind. Although we speak regularly about strategic, incremental changes, this is not about tinkering at the edges. Our goal is to support meaningful change at scale. Ultimately, blended learning is about reinventing what learning looks like for students, and even schools. The schools that win today are the ones that build cultures of sustained learning and innovation across all levels and stakeholder groups. In blended learning terms, winning does not require that other schools lose. In fact, because of the inherent network effects of blended learning, the more schools that build cultures of learning and innovation, the more the collective tide will rise. Through sustained innovation shared over time, transformation is not only possible, it is inevitable.

The seismic shift that education is experiencing demands proactive planning, design, and implementation that is also systemic in nature. It is no longer enough for one progressive teacher to "get it," because then the only students who benefit are the ones lucky enough to be in that teacher's class. It is no longer enough for principals, superintendents, and other school leaders to maintain the status quo. All stakeholders must be engaged and involved in the process of shifting behaviors, practices, and culture.

This chapter

- explains the hallmarks of blended learning;
- describes the importance of culture to the success of an organization;

- explores the unique characteristics of a blended learning culture;

- identifies the key stakeholders who should be involved and considered in a blended learning transformation; and

- discusses why this transformation is so important right now.

CLEARING UP BLENDED LEARNING CONFUSION

There are many definitions of blended learning. The most frequently referenced comes from a nonprofit, nonpartisan think tank, the Christensen Institute, which states,

> Blended Learning is a formal education program in which a student learns: (1) at least in part through online learning, with some element of student control over time, place, path, and/or pace; (2) at least in part in a supervised brick-and-mortar location away from home; (3) and the modalities along each student's learning path within a course or subject are connected to provide an integrated learning experience.

Sometimes the conversation about blended learning includes references to personalized learning, digital learning, 21st-century learning, and next generation classrooms.

The purpose of this book is not to create a new definition. The evolving nature of technology and its potential application mandates a dynamic and similarly evolving understanding of "blended learning." Instead, we remain practical, providing readers with scalable classroom practices and examples of theory in action. When successfully implemented, blended learning enables these hallmarks of best teaching and learning practices:

- **Personalization:** providing unique learning pathways for individual students

- **Agency:** giving learners opportunities to participate in key decisions in their learning experience

- **Authentic Audience:** giving learners the opportunity to create for a real audience both locally and globally

- **Connectivity:** giving learners opportunities to experience learning in collaboration with peers and experts locally and globally

- **Creativity:** providing learners individual and collaborative opportunities to make things that matter while building skills for their future

The goal of this book is to help educators blend the tools and modalities at their disposal to facilitate the best instruction to meet individual student learning needs. The blended learning models presented here are frameworks and starting points, not end points. Ideally, schools become true learning communities capable of adapting approaches and models to meet their unique needs. This book is designed to provide a foundation so that educators can make the right decisions for the needs of their unique instructional environments.

IT STARTS WITH CULTURE

Business management guru Peter Drucker is credited with the phrase, "culture eats strategy for breakfast." This is not to say that strategy isn't important but instead to emphasize that the culture of an organization is the first and greatest determinant of the success or failure of that organization and any initiative that it undertakes. Culture can be described in a number of ways:

- The operationalizing of an organization's values (Aulet, 2014). A balanced blend of human psychology, attitudes, actions, and beliefs that combined create either pleasure or pain, serious momentum or miserable stagnation. (Parr, 2012)

- A system of shared assumptions, values, and beliefs, which governs how people behave in organizations. (McLaughlin, 2016)

- The way that an organization and its people do things and how they feel when they are doing them.

The common theme of any definition of culture is that it is based on shared values, created and perpetuated by people. These values, attitudes, and beliefs combine to yield patterns of behavior, and consequently impact how stakeholders feel about these behaviors. Heath and Heath assert that behavior is contagious particularly in ambiguous situations and "people look to others for cues about how to interpret the event" (Heath & Heath, 2010, p. 226). Leaders managing a blended learning change initiative must be aware of this and align individual and group motivation and rationale with a climate and conditions that support the desired change. Heath and Heath refer to this process in three parts: 1) Directing the rider—providing clear rationale and direction, 2) Motivating the elephant—inspiring feeling and desire to change, and 3) Shaping the path—building the culture and conditions (Heath & Heath, 2010).

Steve Wilcox, CEO of Aspire Public Schools, describes the Aspire culture as one of *confident humility.*

> We're confident enough to try new things and not worry too much that we'll be criticized or penalized too harshly for failure or a drop

in results. We're confident enough to know we are not the experts, but we know some things that position us well to try, learn, fail, and try again. We're confident enough to say: "We're doing this our way, at a pace that fits our culture, and aligned with our mission as an organization." At the same time, we are also humble enough to know we learn everyday from other educators, schools, and systems in powerful ways. We're humble enough to sit and learn from (and with) others who are struggling through the same challenges or who are kind enough to help us even when the issues we're struggling to solve are ones they've solved long ago. (Arney, 2015, p. xiii)

This sentiment is critical for blended learning schools to risk trying new things while remaining open to learning and honoring their unique strengths and challenges.

A BLENDED LEARNING CULTURE

In a blended learning culture, stakeholders are empowered to take greater ownership of their respective responsibilities. Students become agents and owners of their learning process. In the Summit Schools (a nonprofit network of innovative, blended public high schools) this can be observed with daily project time, where students explore real-world projects as problem-solvers and innovators and often present their own findings, analyses, and recommendations. In the blended learning hubs at Rio Vista Middle School in California, teachers outline learning objectives and students choose their learning path based on their interests. In blended learning schools, schooling does not happen *to* students. Students are *drivers* of their learning, even at early ages. Simultaneously, schools, district leaders, and teachers become both facilitators of student learning *and* 21st-century learners themselves. A blended learning school is a true community of learners who have vested participation in the ultimate manifestation of the learning environment and experience.

Providing each stakeholder with a voice and a role yields greater ownership and engagement. In a conversation with veteran superintendent Rick Miller, he explained that building culture is the most critical role of the superintendent and that "we have to give teachers opportunities and incentives to move toward a freer and more democratic environment. . . . We need to disrupt the culture of compliance and create one of professionalism and innovation" (Rick Miller, personal conversation, January 28, 2016). The most effective blended learning initiatives occur with all levels of stakeholder groups engaged and moving in concert. This alignment is achieved by building a cohesive vision—which is where the process starts. Table 1.1 explores the roles of stakeholder groups vital to the success of the blended learning transformation.

TABLE 1.1 Stakeholders and Their Roles

STAKEHOLDER	ROLE
District Leadership	Lead visioning process. Set and model the culture and priorities for the district and ensure that resources (personnel, financial, technological) are in place for success. Establish collective culture and buy-in.
School Leadership	Align the school vision with the district's broader vision and achieve buy-in and engagement among teachers and other staff. Ensure school is properly equipped with the resources necessary for success. Build school-level plan. Commit to a personal development plan to grow skills and proficiency in blended learning and change management.
Teachers	Align school and district vision with class vision. Build buy-in among students and parents. Commit to a personal development plan to grow skills and proficiency in blended learning.
IT Team	Ensure the school and district is equipped with the technology infrastructure to handle the growing tech needs. Work in tandem with the instructional team to anticipate and quickly solve critical tech issues.
Students	Begin to take greater ownership in their learning process as agents. Be respectful to their community as digital citizens and responsible in caring for their new tools.
Parents	Encourage and support the learning and growth of their students through the blended learning transition. Engage constructively in the transition process.

WHERE THE WORLD IS GOING: OUR STUDENTS ARE ALREADY THERE

We are at the moment in education when our schools can determine if they are Netflix or Blockbuster, Amazon or Borders, Samsung or Blackberry. In each of these cases, the successful organization saw that the entire world was changing and decided they were going to change to be ready for it. The failed organizations had, to their detriment, histories and inertias of people that were used to doing things the way they had always been done. This prevented them from shifting vision and culture at the time when it was most critical to their survival. Most realized their error too late while their successors were building nimble learning organizations ready and positioned for where the world was going, and even helped to shape it.

We now have much more than a glimpse of where education is going. Later in Chapter 12, we discuss how a teenager, Logan LaPlante, learned to "hack

> A world of unique hackers is emerging and schools will need to learn how to be flexible enough to adapt and change to facilitate learning in a way that meets the hacker's curious mind. #BLinAction

school." He is not alone in his propensity toward hacking. It represents the desire for today's learners to learn, create, and connect on their own terms, with their own interests, and by their own design. Author Will Richardson describes a conversation with Larry Rosenstock, founder of High Tech High, during a visit to the school: "Larry said, 'We have to stop delivering the curriculum to kids. We have to start discovering it with them . . . especially now, when curriculum is everywhere'" (Richardson, 2012). Children today are communicating to us through the hours they spend designing their own worlds in Minecraft, through new languages they are building with emojis and symbols, by short-circuiting "no phone" policies through iMessage on their 1:1 school-provided devices. In some ways, a world of unique hackers is emerging and schools will need to learn how to be flexible enough to adapt and change to facilitate learning in a way that meets the hacker's curious mind.

This is a big shift for most schools, but adopting the blended learning culture, practices, and approaches can be the bridge. Ironically, most schools were designed to help students learn, but they were not designed to learn themselves. The blended learning school is designed both to learn and facilitate learning. This ongoing organizational learning is critical as students are learning technology at younger ages, technology tools are evolving, and requisite skills for success in the marketplace are shifting.

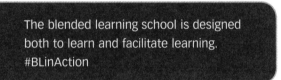

The blended learning school is designed both to learn and facilitate learning. #BLinAction

K–12 education stands at its greatest inflection point—a collision course with irrelevance, or the opportunity for reinvention. By the actions and decisions it makes over the next few years, each district, each school, each teacher will choose whether to meet the needs of today's learners or not.

WRAPPING IT UP

Austrian neurologist, psychiatrist, and Holocaust survivor Viktor Frankl stated, "Between stimulus and response there is a space. In that space is our power to choose our response. In our response lies our growth and our freedom." In this era of rapid change, the stimuli are seemingly infinite. It can feel impossible to create the space described by Frankl in order to bring intention and true choice to the path forward. Schools are not exempt from the pitfalls that can result from failure to create this space when considering blended learning models. There have been many failed attempts as a result of hasty reactive decisions in the face of trends or pressure to improve.

At the same time, space does not mean long-term immobility or inertia. Instead, the space necessary to wisely choose the response to the frenetic stimuli of change is one of awareness of one's landscape and stakeholders. In this space, the focus is on generating shared vision, developing a 360 degree perspective, encouraging stakeholder voice, and designing an iterative practice. By nurturing a positive blended learning culture and engaging stakeholders in actualizing the shared vision, leaders can more confidently take the first steps in their blended learning journeys.

BOOK STUDY QUESTIONS

1. Think about where you are starting this journey. Based on the definition of blended learning, are there any blended learning practices already in place in your school? Discuss how blended learning differs from technology integration.

2. To what extent are you able to currently personalize, help your students connect with other peers or teachers outside their classroom, enable students to have some control over "time, place, path, or pace," and allow students to create using technology tools?

3. What are the current organizational beliefs, values, and attitudes toward technology and blended learning within your school's culture?

4. Thinking about each stakeholder group's shared attitudes, values, and beliefs: from your stakeholder vantage point, how could you influence other stakeholders to cultivate positive shared attitudes, values, and beliefs?

5. Looking at this book's table of Contents, what are you most excited to learn about? Discuss with your group a strategy for reading this book. Will you proceed in order or in a nonlinear fashion based on key interest points? Get excited to share this journey together!

CHAPTER 2

Getting Started

I love learning when there is a ton of interaction whether it is teacher to student or student to student making it easy to see other points of view besides your own.

—Victoria Sandoval, 9th Grade

Though sometimes daunting, a thoughtful blended learning transformation is not only worth the time, energy, and effort, but necessary to keep pace with the rapidly evolving education landscape. The initial steps of getting started are absolutely critical to the long-term success of the blended learning initiative. Whether a school has already begun experimenting or has fully launched a blended initiative, it is not too late to implement these best practices.

This chapter

- introduces the *Blended Learning Roadmap: The Pathway to Personalization* (Figure 2.1, courtesy of Redbird Advanced Learning);

- explains the elements of Phase 1 of a blended learning initiative—Building the Foundation;

- illustrates the collective visioning process and its importance in authentically engaging the community of stakeholders;

- discusses the critical elements of the assessment process and how to determine the classroom, school, or district's readiness; and

- describes the characteristics that should be evident in newly transitioning blended classrooms.

First and foremost, we highly recommend an incremental process as illustrated in Figure 2.1, the *Blended Learning Roadmap*.

In most cases, the complete shift to blended learning may require anywhere from three to five years; however, much progress can be made in even one year with the right planning. The timeframe for a blended learning initiative depends on the starting characteristics of a given school or district, and the

FIGURE 2.1 Blended Learning Roadmap: The Pathway to Personalization

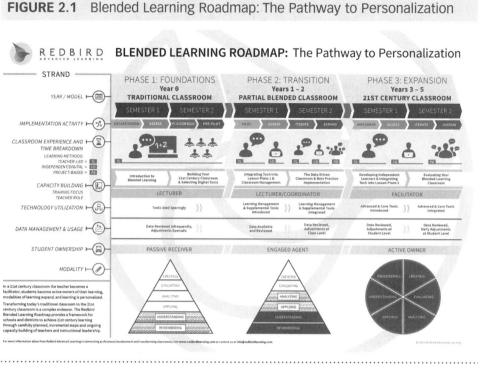

Courtesy of Redbird Advanced Learning.

scale and scope of the blended learning vision. There may be unique challenges with regard to infrastructure, technology, staff proficiency, or other unique characteristics. This is okay. More important than transforming overnight is setting off in the right direction with key players sharing the same vision and working together. The *Blended Learning Roadmap* outlines the key phases of a blended learning transformation: **Phase 1: Foundations, Phase 2: Transitions, Phase 3: Expansion.**

PHASE 1: BUILDING THE FOUNDATION

This chapter focuses on **Phase 1: Foundations** to illustrate the elements that help ensure the blended learning implementation starts on the right path, and at the right pace. The processes for leaders and classroom teachers are very similar and ideally should happen in tandem. There are several moving pieces, and each piece needs to be well thought out to help secure the overall success of the initiative.

Stage 1: Engagement and Vision—Cohesion of Vision and Pedagogy

As with any new project, organization, or initiative, a blended learning implementation should start with a clear and cohesive vision and purpose.

In *Go Blended,* Liz Arney recommends that schools "hire technology to help solve one of your pressing instructional problems, not for technology's sake" (Arney, 2015, p. 20). Remaining steadfast on the instructional problem increases discipline and focus. Forming a clear vision does not mean that everything needs to be figured out from the beginning. In fact, it is unrealistic to expect definitive solutions at the onset because the program will evolve with increasing proficiency, technology advancements, and trial and error. The visioning process also serves to establish buy-in and engagement from key stakeholders. The earlier and more often that key people are brought into the process, the greater likelihood that they take ownership and feel like authentic participants.

Authentic Participants

An effective approach to visioning is to include key stakeholders as *authentic participants* in the process. Authentic participation involves the incorporation of the voices, opinions, needs, and concerns of participants in a meaningful way. Stakeholders become quickly disillusioned if they are asked to participate in these early conversations, but do not feel genuinely heard or valued. Figure 2.2 shows the progression of the collective visioning process.

The visioning process can take the form of a single meeting, or series of meetings using a combination of in-person and virtual formats. The key is to invest enough time and quality interaction to generate buy-in and build cohesion. Additionally, the shared vision creates a common bond among the group when problems or differences of opinion arise. Planning is intentionally not included in the visioning process. Developing a shared vision allows for a smaller committee to build a preliminary plan and present back to

FIGURE 2.2 Visioning Process

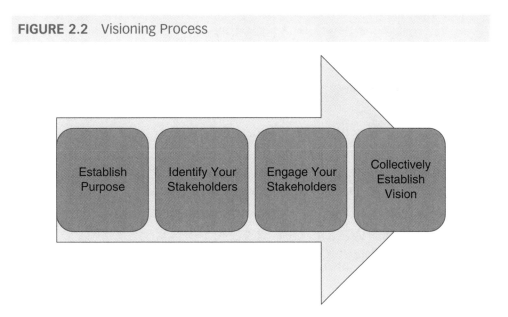

TABLE 2.1 Visioning Process

VISIONING PROCESS	LEADERS	TEACHERS
Establish Purpose—Understand why you are taking on this blended learning initiative	Why are you embarking on this initiative? Are you trying to stay relevant with changing times? Are you seeking to address academic challenges? Are you trying to make your school and students more 21st-century ready?	What instructional problem(s) are you trying to solve? What are the academic needs of your students? Are you trying to address classroom management challenges?
Identify your Stakeholders—Who are the people/groups you must get on board?	A school/district leader must think broadly about stakeholders in a blended learning initiative. As the bulk of the heavy lifting takes place inside the classrooms, principals, teachers, students, and parents must be proactively engaged and onboard.	Teachers must think strategically about the support they need to get their blended learning initiative off the ground—specifically from the principal or school leadership, other teachers, and the tech team. The teacher must also consider how to engage the students and parents in the process.
Understand What Matters to Key Stakeholders—What are the needs and interests of different groups?	The engagement process for leaders should start early in the blended learning initiative. It is key to get opinions, feedback, and concerns from stakeholders using both formal and informal processes.	Teachers should understand the needs of their students and parents to ensure that they are meeting these stakeholders where they are.
Collectively Establish Vision—How do we get everyone moving in the same direction?	The ultimate vision of the initiative is most powerful when incorporating the voice and needs of key stakeholder groups.	The classroom vision should be a collective process, including input from students (and, where possible, parents) regarding their needs, goals, and desires for their learning experience.

the visioning group. Planning is a significantly more concrete process that requires a deeper and more intense focus.

Stage 2: Assess–What Is Our Starting Point?

With more examples of lessons learned from districts across the country, organizations like *Education Elements* and others are helping to bring best practice thinking and processes to the blended learning transformation process. One of these best practices is conducting a thorough assessment at the onset. In the assessment phase, it is important to understand the school or district's true starting point. In most cases, this is somewhere in Phase 1: Foundations of the *Blended Learning Roadmap*. Schools that have already set off on a blended path may be approaching, or in, Phase 2: Transitions. In either case, there is usually some level of blended instruction taking place on a small scale, or there is somewhat spotty implementation on a larger scale. Most likely, some teachers have started to engage in some level of technology integration, but are unsure of the fidelity of the implementation or are looking to strengthen their practice.

The assessment phase helps to ensure that the starting point, path, and pace of the transition is fitting for a given school or district. Not investing the required time and resources into the assessment may result in moving too quickly or too slowly into the initiative, or making wrong instructional decisions. These misestimations can lead to wasted time, money, and energy as seen most notoriously with the Los Angeles Unified School District iPad initiative of 2013, where the district ambitiously began supplying all students with iPads only to quickly halt the program due to curricular, technological, and personnel unpreparedness.

In the assessment phase, four key factors should be considered to determine the readiness of a district, school, or classroom for blended learning:

1. School/District Culture

2. Staff Proficiency (Leadership and Teacher Capacity)

3. Current Instructional Program

4. Technology Infrastructure

As described below, these factors are the same for leaders and teachers only applied in different ways.

Culture

LEADERS	TEACHERS
Understand the existing culture of their school or district, the current operational and emotional behaviors and feelings of key stakeholders. • Are principals and teachers eager to lead and be part of a change initiative? • Are teachers feeling energized to try new things?	Understand the existing school and classroom culture. • Are students eager and ready to learn? • Are parents supportive? • How do students feel about change and integration of new tools? • How do students define "good teaching" and "good learning"?

Proficiency

LEADERS	TEACHERS
Understand the current skill level of staff as it relates to technology integration in classrooms and learning.	Understand the current skill and readiness of their students.
<ul><li>Do school leadership teams have the capacity and skill to manage a change initiative?</li><li>Where are teachers in their current meaningful usage of technology? Are they able to identify and apply technology tools effectively for instruction? What is their frequency of usage in the classroom?</li></ul>	<ul><li>What technology proficiencies do they possess and which ones do they need?</li><li>Do students understand how to interact positively and productively with each other in a discussion, interpret data to track their progress, transition between activities smoothly?</li></ul>

Academic Program

LEADERS	TEACHERS
Assess the current academic program strengths and pedagogical models to plan for incremental change.	Determine the current strengths of their current classroom practice.
<ul><li>What is happening in classrooms now?</li><li>Where are there opportunities for quick victories via small changes first?</li><li>What teachers could be galvanized as teacher trailblazers?</li></ul>	<ul><li>What units/activities could be slightly modified to incorporate blended practices?</li><li>What blended learning model offers incremental progress?</li><li>What activities would acculturate students to new learning styles?</li></ul>

Technology Infrastructure

LEADERS	TEACHERS
Assess the current technology infrastructure: Wi-Fi, devices, furniture, outlets, and bandwidth.	Assess what is currently available.
<ul><li>What options are truly available to the school immediately and over time?</li><li>What purchases or adjustments that exceed existing capacity are necessary for successful implementation so as to avoid disgruntled teachers, students, and parents?</li></ul>	<ul><li>What resources are available in the classroom and throughout the school?</li><li>What technology do students have access to, and would the school support BYOD (bring your own device) practices for use of personal devices?</li></ul>

Understanding these elements helps leaders and teachers make smart decisions for Phase 1. Many schools or districts opt to hire outside firms to conduct a full assessment of blended learning readiness while others conduct a more internally driven process. Though there are positives and negatives to each path, the key is to ensure an honest process that yields accurate data and findings.

An honest assessment serves as insurance to help a district or school avoid making overly ambitious and often costly leaps from their existing structure, or pushing people faster than their mindset or current capacity allows them to go. Honesty in the assessment phase should be tempered

> The key is to ensure an honest assessment process that yields accurate data and findings of the school or district's blended learning readiness. #BLinAction

with compassion. Mike Ritzius, co-founder of the EdCamp Foundation and Associate Director of Professional Development for New Jersey Education Association, speaks of the importance of "honoring and respecting the people who paved the way for current innovators" (Mike Ritzius, personal communication, January 9, 2016). The shift to blended learning represents big leaps that can put significant strain on systems, leaders, and teachers. It is important to value the foundational work, people, and existing strengths during periods of change and innovation.

LINKS TO THE CLASSROOM: PARTICIPATING IN DISCUSSIONS ABOUT MINDSET

Teachers should make a point to include themselves in conversations about culture, staff proficiency, academic programs, and technology infrastructure. They should have a clear vision of where both they and their students are beginning this journey. For many teachers, transitioning to a blended learning model requires a radical shift in their perception of their role as the teacher in the classroom as well as their students' roles as learners in the classroom. This shift in role is also experienced by students who may have a preexisting expectation of teacher and student roles that are different from those in a blended model.

Start the conversation about mindset with your school leadership, your peers, and your students. Figure 2.3 provides an idea of the types of shifts teachers should be contemplating as they set off on their blended learning journey.

- How do you and your students see the teacher-student roles in your classroom right now?

- How are you and your students currently using technology in your classroom?

- Have you used the SAMR (Substitution, Augmentation, Modification, Redefinition) or TPACK (Technological Pedagogical Content Knowledge) model to identify the role of technology in your lessons? What routines or class norms do you have in place to ensure that students are using technology responsibly (e.g., class contract)?

- If you could redesign your classroom, what would it look like?

FIGURE 2.3 Phase 1 in Shifting to Blended Learning Classroom

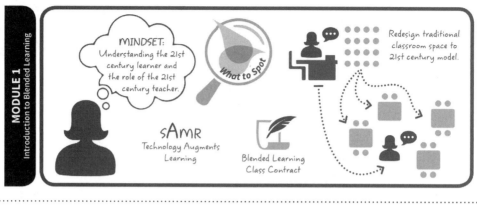

Courtesy of Redbird Advanced Learning.

Stage 3: Planning and Design

The collective vision and data gathered from the assessment phase informs the blended learning plan and design. The plan incorporates the timeframe, the resources and people to be employed, and the activities. Planning a 1:1 initiative is very different than planning a BYOD or classroom rotation. Determining the design is therefore embedded into the planning phase to ensure proper alignment and goal setting. Allocate approximately six months to one year for the Phase 1 process of a blended initiative.

The key design elements to consider in transitioning to blended learning include a digital content strategy, digital apps and tools strategy, instructional delivery model, and the professional development plan and model. Table 2.2 helps leaders and teachers think through key decisions involving each element. These elements comprehensively form the overall blended learning design and help ensure cohesion. Each of these elements is outlined in greater detail throughout the book.

Stage 4: Pre-Pilot

The final important stage for phase 1 is the pre-pilot. We do not yet consider this a pilot because this is a designed opportunity to fail small and fail fast, adapt quickly, and learn from mistakes. A small group of teachers and schools can begin to implement blended learning in a portion of their classrooms to test for challenges, such as technology limitations, teacher readiness, student readiness, ease of onboarding, to name a few. By having this dry run (which may not last more than two to three months), many of the inevitable bugs in the system emerge and leaders can see where things need to be tightened up or adjusted prior to the pilot. Rio Public Schools in

TABLE 2.2 Design Elements

DESIGN ELEMENT	DECISION
Digital Content	What are the key content areas you want the digital instruction to focus on? Are there specific grade levels? Are there specific groups of students that you want to target?
Digital Apps and Tools	How do you want digital technology to impact the learning experience? Are you looking to achieve greater student engagement? Address classroom management issues? Give students greater opportunities to connect? To explore? To communicate?
Instructional Delivery	What do you want the classroom experience to be? How much control/ownership do you want to give to the students? How does this align to the readiness of your teachers?
Professional Development	How can staff (school leaders and teachers) become 21st-century learners and educators? How can professional development be integrated, prioritized, and personalized to meet the needs of all learners (school leaders and teachers)?

Oxnard, California, created the Rio Lab Class (@riolabclass) that is essentially an ongoing pre-pilot. The lab class helps teachers experiment with innovations in blended learning with the expectation that some will succeed and many will fail. The lab class is a student favorite with its special focus on student-driven and project-based learning. Promising approaches are further tested and oftentimes expanded to other classrooms in the district. Teachers often observe the lab class for ideas and learning. Table 2.3 compares the pre-pilot to the actual pilot. The pre-pilot phase is distinct from a pilot in some important ways.

TABLE 2.3 Characteristics of the Pre-Pilot Versus Pilot

PRE-PILOT	PILOT
Expect to fail	Hoping to succeed
Smaller in scale	Large enough in scale to produce usable data
Goal is to surface kinks in the system	Goal is to surface a usable model and approach for expansion
Identify implementation challenges	Measure for results
Assess value or fit	Test quality of value, fit, and effectiveness

Identifying and Enlisting Pre-Pilot Teachers

The pre-pilot is a great opportunity for teachers to get involved in the shift to a blended learning model early in the process. The pre-pilot teachers are usually early adopters who are already using technology with their students. Leaders can handpick these teachers, but it may be more equitable to present the opportunity to the whole staff and ask interested teachers to participate. Broward County Public Schools in Florida used a preliminary technology readiness assessment to identify technology advanced teachers and invited them to participate in professional development in personalized blended learning. Over 300 teachers across eighty schools volunteered and are now the beginning of organic growth of blended learning in the district. Districts can also ask teachers to complete an informal application with the following questions:

- Why do you want to participate in the pre-pilot? What do you hope to learn in this process?

- How are you currently using technology?

- Thinking about the SAMR/TPACK model, where would you say most of your lessons currently are—substitution, augmentation, modification or redefinition?

- How do you want digital technology to impact the learning experience?

- Are you willing to spend time attending professional development opportunities and collaborating with other pre-pilot teachers?

The answers to these questions will provide insight into teachers' thoughts on technology as well as their motivation for joining the pre-pilot. In addition to an informal application, it's helpful to conduct short observations of the teachers who expressed interest to make sure you are selecting a strong group of teachers. It's important that these teachers are willing to invest time and energy into this process. They need to be open-minded, willing to experiment, and able to roll with technology bumps as they attempt to shift to a blended learning model.

LINKS TO THE CLASSROOM: ENGAGING STUDENT VOICE IN PRE-PILOTS

As students engage in Pre-pilots, it is helpful for them to also have an understanding of what they can expect during this phase. By including students in an ongoing conversation about their role in a blended classroom, teachers can avoid student frustration from any "kinks" as they are worked out, and can engage students as participants in assessing the value of the program. This is accomplished within a pre-pilot group of students during the onboarding process, which we further discuss in Chapter 8. As part of the "defining" component of onboarding, teachers can inform students of the following expectations:

- We have an important role in determining whether this new digital tool is a good learning resource for more students here at the school.

- We need your help in assessing whether this is going to be valuable to the program, so be ready to provide feedback along the way . . . don't be shy!

- Since this is our first time using this tool(s), we'll probably encounter a few "fail-forward" moments where things don't work out exactly as planned. These moments are very important to help us learn.

- I'll count on you to help us work out the kinks together and make recommendations whether we use this tool(s) for more students or not.

WRAPPING IT UP

Whether you want to improve on an existing implementation or are truly just getting started in your blended learning journey, you are not too late to implement these important best practices in getting started. The keys are to be honest about where you are; do not bite off more than you can chew; build on your strengths; and think incrementally. The getting started process involves the following four elements.

- **Engaging and Visioning:** Identify your key stakeholders and involve them in the process of developing a shared vision.

- **Assessment:** Understand your current starting point so that you can determine the pace and path of your blended learning plan.

- **Planning and Design:** Develop your plan based on the knowledge gained in the assessment process.

- **Pre-pilot:** Fail fast and learn by trying something small. Tease out the needs and foreseeable hurdles before you contemplate your larger rollout.

BOOK STUDY QUESTIONS

1. Who are your key stakeholders and what is your plan to meaningfully engage them in the visioning process?

2. How would you describe the existing culture in your district, school, or classroom?

3. What are the key strengths you expect to build on from the assessment phase? What are the key limitations or challenges you expect to learn?

4. What is your predominant current instructional model?

5. How can you structure your pre-pilot to fail fast and still obtain key learnings?

CHAPTER 3

The Blended Learning Elements of Effectiveness

I feel that I like using technology to learn because you have this kind of independent feeling and you feel in control. I like this because we are learning and having fun and what's learning without the fun?

—Fiona Lui Martin, 4th Grade

The Blended Learning Elements of Effectiveness tool pictured in Figure 3.1 (courtesy of Redbird Advanced Learning) codifies the essential elements of an effective blended learning initiative, helps ensure cohesion of planning and vision, and provides a tool for continued assessment and iteration. Similar to the empowerment evaluation model (Clinton & Hattie, 2014), the framework increases the capacity of stakeholders to "plan, implement, and evaluate their own programmes thus increasing the likelihood of success" (Hattie, 2015, p. 23). The Elements of Effectiveness tool is intentionally cyclical in nature, since the blended learning process is more iterative than linear and should continue to improve and build on itself as instructional staff become more proficient and obtain more data points about what is working at the district, school, and classroom level. Additionally, the process is interconnected in that each element impacts the others; however, there is a way to approach the process with some degree of sequence for planning and structure. The cycle progresses in the following order: 1. Visioning, 2. Capacity Building, 3. Technology Utilization, 4. Data Management, and 5. Student Ownership.

This chapter

- dissects the critical elements that ultimately drive the success or failure of a blended learning initiative; and

- emphasizes each element's usefulness for instructional leadership to initiate and manage a comprehensive blended learning initiative.

FIGURE 3.1 The Blended Learning Elements of Effectiveness

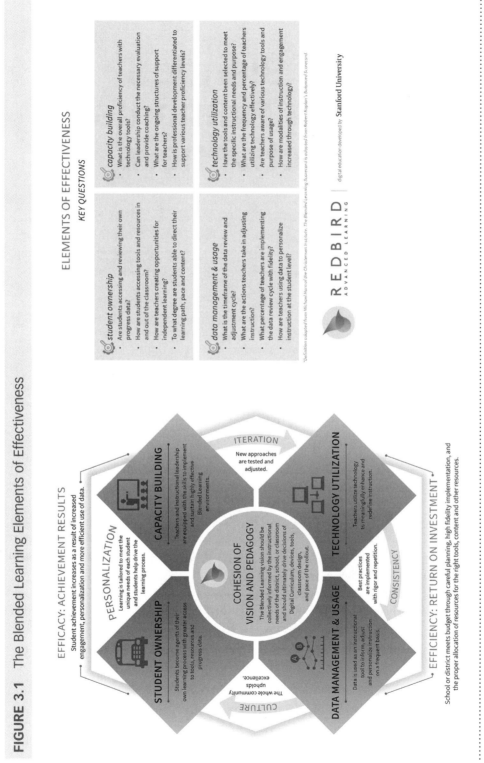

Courtesy of Redbird Advanced Learning.

Throughout the book, the Elements of Effectiveness are referenced and identified by icon, demonstrating the need to remain comprehensive in the planning, implementation, and evaluation of the initiative.

THE ELEMENTS DESCRIBED

Cohesion of Vision and Pedagogy

As discussed in Chapter 2, the blended learning initiative should start with a collective vision informed by the instructional needs of the district, school, or classroom. This vision should ultimately drive decisions of digital curriculum, devices, tools, classroom design, and pace of the rollout. Each blended learning model presents unique pedagogical opportunities. To achieve cohesion of school vision and pedagogy, school leaders should strive to match the teaching practices embedded in each model to the school's academic goals and practices. For example, a school that prioritizes collaboration and project-based learning can find cohesion in a rotation station practice in which one of the stations is dedicated to small group projects.

 ## Capacity Building: Teachers and Instructional Leadership Are Equipped With the Skills to Implement and Sustain Highly Effective Blended Environments

Fullan and Quinn describe collective capacity building as "the increased ability of educators at all levels of the system to make the instructional changes required to raise the bar and close the gap for all students" (Fullan & Quinn, 2016, p. 57). One of the greatest challenges of a blended learning initiative is that the teachers, leaders, and students are learning new skills together. This new paradigm can be very unsettling for instructional leaders and teachers, create anxiety, and even impede experimentation and innovation. On the other hand, Richardson in his Ted Talk explains, "People who model their own learning process [are able to] connect to other learners as a regular part of their day, and learn continuously around the things they have a passion for" (Richardson, 2012).

Through this opportunity for modeling in a blended learning initiative, the whole school becomes a learning community starting with three key behaviors:

1. **Honesty and humility**—Admitting that you are all learning new skills, tools, and techniques together. This helps create a feeling of safety within the group and allows you to be more reachable for support.

2. **Becoming the lead learner**—According to research conducted by Robinson, Lloyd, and Rowe (2008), the single greatest impact a

school principal can have—by a factor of two—was to participate as a learner in professional development with staff in helping to move the school forward.

3. **Establishing and maintaining structures of support**—This is one of the most important areas where an instructional leader can best support teachers, especially as you are learning together. In the same way, a practicing blended learning teacher becomes a facilitator of learning and not a holder of knowledge, by establishing structures of support you are reducing the need to be the expert of all things blended learning, and helping to ensure that there are structures in place for teachers to continue learning independently and collectively. These types of structures are covered in more detail later in Chapter 4.

Capacity building is the foundation of the blended learning initiative because it develops the culture; accelerates the speed of the change; fosters sustainability; and reinforces the strategy (Fullan & Quinn, 2016).

LINKS TO THE CLASSROOM: BUILDING STUDENT CAPACITY

Taking the time to build technology skills for students is similarly important. The erroneous assumption that teachers sometimes make is that being a digital native means students will pick things up easily and/or without training. Most digital natives have learned to use technology in very specific ways, typically with respect to consumption and social interaction. The reality is that students need just as much onboarding into new technology environments as the teachers, especially as it relates to using technology for instructional purposes. Strategies for onboarding students effectively are covered in Chapter 8.

Technology Utilization: Technology Is Used to Meaningfully Enhance and Redefine Instruction

The presence of technology does not equate to meaningful use or impact in the classroom. A thoughtful approach to the specific technology chosen and how it is deployed is critical. In Chapters 5, 6, and 8 we go into more detail regarding the selection and deployment of the right technology based on pedagogy, learning goals, budget, and other constraints. With adequate capacity building, teachers should be in position to identify and use technology tools to meet their instructional needs. Consequently, this becomes their technology toolbox (Chapter 5).

LINKS TO THE CLASSROOM: GETTING CREATIVE WITH LIMITED RESOURCES

Faced with a frustrating lack of resources and technology, many teachers work creatively to implement blended practices where possible, even without the ideal tools to do the job. If you are teaching in a school where devices and tools are not provided for students, then the question becomes whether personal devices can be leveraged to help students get connected. This may be possible in the following ways:

- Embracing a BYOD (Bring Your Own Device) practice in your class

- Using more blended tools as homework or for out of school activities

- Educating students about local public Wi-Fi access points, such as libraries or cafes

- Connecting low-income families with programs that offer discounted devices and internet

- Engaging local community partners to donate devices

However, it is always important to provide choice for students to work offline if relying on personal access, since unfortunately many students do not have Wi-Fi or device access outside of school.

Data Management and Usage: Data Is Used as an Instructional Tool to Inform, Adjust, and Personalize Instruction on a Frequent Basis

Since leveraging formative data to adjust and personalize instruction is one of the greatest benefits of an effective blended learning initiative, the majority of the data conversation in this book is dedicated to formative assessments. The emergence of technology in classes presents an unprecedented opportunity for teachers to not only obtain data on a more frequent basis, but also to analyze that data, and use it to adjust instruction accordingly. A high-performing blended learning classroom should strive to achieve ongoing data collection and incorporate instructional adjustments at the student level. Furthermore, the type and scope of data obtained can be more holistic thus helping a teacher increase personalization (Chapter 7).

Student Ownership: Students Become Agents of Their Own Learning Process With Greater Access to Tools, Resources, and Progress Data

The height of a blended learning initiative is when the student (or learner) takes ownership of their learning process. However, this doesn't mean that teachers aren't involved. In fact, research shows significant impact on learning when high expectations are set by teachers (Rubie-Davies, 2015) combined with support and opportunities for personalized learning. Student ownership is a critical component of personalization in which "learners first understand how they learn best. Then they acquire the skills to choose and use the tools that work best for their learning qualities" (Bray & McClaskey, 2013, p. 15).

> The height of a blended learning initiative is when the student (or learner) takes ownership of their learning process.
> #BLinAction

Student ownership occurs when the learner actually becomes a self-directing, self-resourcing, self-correcting, and self-reflecting agent in their learning process, as illustrated in Figure 3.2 below. In this manner, the student is an ongoing contributor to the conversation of their learning. Ideally, as students matures they assume an increasing role in this process.

One of the greatest benefits of well integrated technology is that the traditional constraints of a classroom or teacher instruction are removed. Learning is no longer limited to a specific location or a finite amount of time. Through the use and availability of technology tools, students can learn anywhere, at any time, and at the pace and mode that fits their unique needs.

This is a new paradigm of learning that requires a shift in mindset of both the teacher (from lecturer to facilitator) and the student (from passive receiver to active owner). Greater detail on making these shifts is outlined in role definition tables and by the "student ownership" icon throughout the book.

FIGURE 3.2 The Student Ownership Paradigm

SELF-DIRECTING	SELF-RESOURCING	SELF-CORRECTING	SELF-REFLECTING
• Student has input into the content, pace, and structure of the learning process.	• Student has access to resources that can facilitate the learning process and the wherewithal to identify additional resources.	• Student has the self-awareness to reset and reorient path when challenges are confronted by adjusting pace, mode, resource, etc.	• Student assesses the overall process and makes broader iterative adjustments as needed.

WRAPPING IT UP

The blended learning initiative must be viewed, planned, and implemented in a cohesive and comprehensive manner. The Blended Learning Elements of Effectiveness provide a framework so that schools can ensure that the elements critical to success are addressed and assessed. Leaders should view the Blended Learning Elements of Effectiveness as a tool for planning and continued iteration recognizing that the implementation will evolve over time.

BOOK STUDY QUESTIONS

1. How would you describe the current proficiency and readiness of teachers in your school(s) as it relates to blended learning? Are there champions or leaders emerging?

2. What are the structures of support that are already in place for building capacity of teachers in your school(s)? How can you leverage these existing supports in building capacity for blended learning?

3. Which technology tools are currently available to your instructional staff? How effective is the current usage? What evaluation tools are in place or desired to better assess effectiveness?

4. Describe the existing data culture in your school(s). How frequent are data cycles? Are teachers using data to adjust instruction on a personalized level?

5. To what degree do students take ownership of their learning? What are some success stories of student ownership? How can these be replicated?

CHAPTER 4

Preparing Teachers for Blended Instruction

Teaching and learning isn't a one-way street. It is dynamic and flows both ways between student and teacher.

—Conor Brown, 10th Grade

Renowned researcher and learning scientist Dr. Arnetha F. Ball of Stanford University developed the Model of Generative Change for professional development based on the fundamental premise that regulations do not transform schools and teaching, but rather critical thinking, continuous learning with students and from students, and generativity in teachers' thinking and practices transforms schools and teaching. She explains that teachers are not *objects* of change, they are *agents* of change. One of the greatest challenges facing schools in delivering successful blended learning instruction is properly and effectively preparing teachers. In blended instruction, teachers implement a host of new instructional skills, strategies, and technology tools. They must rethink their role in the classroom to transition from owners of information to facilitators of learning. This requires teachers to expand their view of where and how learning happens and what the term "classroom" even means. Technology means little if this shift does not occur. As such, effective professional development may be the most important aspect of achieving a successful blended learning initiative.

> Teachers are not objects of change. They are agents of change.—Dr. Arnetha Ball, Stanford University #BLinAction

A recent study by the Bill & Melinda Gates Foundation found that only twenty-nine percent of teachers are highly satisfied with current professional development offerings, and a large majority of teachers do not believe that professional development is helping to prepare them for the changing nature of their jobs (Boston Counseling Group, 2014). Most professional development is wasting teachers' valuable time.

Sadly, this is not news to any experienced educator. This problem is exacerbated in the professional development of blended learning because these new approaches and skills are not small shifts in instructional practice. We are asking teachers to make big leaps; to dramatically adjust their practices; to incorporate new tools; and reimagine what teaching and learning look like. Furthermore, this shift is not subject or grade specific. Every teacher needs this exposure so any solution needs to be scalable and affordable. This creates an immediate challenge because most districts do not have the internal capacity, expertise, nor funding to implement traditional solutions at scale. There are possibilities, however, and many districts are creatively overcoming these obstacles.

This chapter

- illustrates the best practices of highly effective professional development to prepare teachers for blended learning;

- provides guiding principles and a framework for planning and organizing effective blended learning professional development; and

- provides recommendations on how schools can differentiate and even personalize professional development to better meet the unique needs of teachers at various stages of blended learning readiness and proficiency.

As illustrated in the *Blended Learning Roadmap,* capacity building is an ongoing process with a goal of moving teachers from traditional lecturers to 21st-century facilitators.

 ## WHAT WORKS IN PROFESSIONAL DEVELOPMENT

Conclusive research into the best practices of professional development is very difficult to obtain because very few research studies have been conducted that are able to isolate specific variables of effectiveness. In a recent study of effective professional development for blended and 21st-century classrooms conducted by researchers at the Stanford Graduate School of Education, four key promising practices emerged:

1. **Duration and distribution:** professional development should span longer periods of time (some studies indicating 14+ hours broken up into smaller segments)

2. **Coaching and collaboration:** ongoing, iterative coaching and collaboration between teachers and coaches with observations, feedback, planning, and data analysis

3. **Simulation of practice:** role-playing activities and active learning where teachers have opportunities to practice and apply learnings

4. **Technology:** well-designed interactive digital learning experiences can be as effective as in-person methods and provide personalization for pace, content, and readiness. (Ball, 2015)

This research points to the need for schools to fundamentally rethink how most professional development is delivered in order to embed it into regular practice over time, include coaching and collaboration, and provide regular opportunities for teachers to simulate practice. This helps create not just a community of learning, but a community of learners. The finding that technology can serve as an effective modality of professional development is encouraging as it supports the overall blended approach while increasing opportunities for scale and cost management.

Guiding Principle of Blended Learning Professional Development #1: As the Student, So the Teacher (CHOMP)

Recently, the *personalized learning* movement has inundated the education world. While there is a significant push to creatively differentiate and personalize student-facing instruction, we are just starting to take up the same cause for teachers in a meaningful way. Educators, such as Randall Sampson, Jason Bretzman, Kenny Bosch, and others are helping to create new frameworks and approaches to personalize professional development, and are using Twitter to further the conversation at #PersonalizedPD. Redbird Advanced Learning partnered with Stanford University's Graduate School of Education to create a personalized professional learning platform where teachers can learn at their own pace, choose their own path, and collaborate with other educators with similar learning objectives.

> We must allow teachers to become the 21st-century learners that we are asking them to help create. #BLinAction

The goal of these efforts is to allow teachers to trade places with the blended learner in order to experience the benefits of these practices firsthand, thus becoming the 21st-century learners that we are asking them to help create. This is accomplished by infusing what we call the CHOMP framework— Collaboration, Hands-on learning, Ongoing experiences, Mindset shifts, and Personalization—into professional development.

Collaborate: Coach, and Create Meaningful Connections

In his book, *The Innovator's Mindset,* George Couros says that the three most important words in education are *relationships, relationships, relationships*. This is especially critical in blended learning environments where connections are fundamental. Couros explains,

Rather than limiting educators' initiative, and thereby students' learning opportunities, let's create environments of competitive collaboration, where educators at all levels push and help one another to become better. . . . We must build and strengthen relationships with (and between) our educators so that every individual sees him or herself as an integral part of a larger whole. (Couros, 2015, Kindle Location 1048 of 3535)

If you ask most teachers how they prefer to learn, their first response is *from other teachers*. This is an understanding that organizations like Edcamp are validating and building on by providing vehicles where teachers can share and discuss challenges and ideas that are important to them. Edcamp started in May 2010, and since then there are over 1,000 edcamps in all 50 states and across 26 continents. Other models are emerging, such as the "Pineapple Chart" method explained by Mark Barnes and Jennifer Gonzalez in their book *Hacking Education,* "a systematic way to put a 'welcome mat' out for all classrooms, a central message board that lets other teachers know that you're doing something worth watching today, and if they'd like to come by, your door is open" (Barnes & Gonzalez, 2015), and the Teachers' Guild by Ideo, a virtual professional community of teachers crowdsourcing education design solutions, found online at www.teachersguild.org. The rapid pace of change and innovation in blended learning further necessitates connection as teachers can learn of new approaches, tools, and strategies from other teachers all the time in real time. Participating in twitter chats like #satchat, #sunchat, #Nt2t (New teachers to Twitter), and #edchat held at scheduled times, or as ongoing conversations can help build your professional learning network (PLN).

The most effective blended learning districts and schools infuse coaching from experts and more experienced blended teachers on a regular basis to help ensure the development of best practices. Tustin Unified School District in California expanded the blended learning capacity of their teachers districtwide by using mentoring exponentially. They started with a group of two teachers who became blended learning experts. Then, each expert coached eight to twelve teachers each year who became fellows. Now in their third year, representing almost half of the teachers in the district, over four hundred teachers have been coached intensely in blended learning. This is a powerful application of professional learning communities (PLCs) and mentor teachers and a great way to achieve the right balance of peer-to-peer and peer-to-expert support.

FIGURE 4.1 The CHOMP Framework to Professional Development

Collaborate ⟩ Hands-on ⟩ Ongoing ⟩ Mindset ⟩ Personalize

LINKS TO THE CLASSROOM: HELP STUDENTS CONNECT

Students find inspiration through connectivity. In fact, social interaction is arguably the greatest motivator driving adolescents. Beyond motivating students, teachers also gain a "sandbox" to model positive and purposeful use of social media when they incorporate connectivity tools into the classroom. Edutopia's *A Guidebook for Social Media in the Classroom,* by Vicki Davis, presents several ideas on how to help students connect, and precautions that teachers should take to ensure the sandbox is safe and supervised.

Vignette: Kerry Gallagher, Blended Learning Teacher and Digital Learning Specialist, Boston, Massachusetts (@kerryhawk02)

As a teacher hungry for a constant source of new ideas to keep my students' learning fresh, I joined a district cohort of fellow educators. We wrote weekly reflections about how we were implementing the instructional practices we learned together. Those write-ups were posted to a closed online course. Only participants had access to it.

After just one post, it felt like something was missing. I worked hard on my reflections. When I'd had a success, I was excited to share it. When I fumbled, I wanted to seek advice from my colleagues. My small cohort was a responsive group, but I knew I could get more feedback if I shared my reflections more widely. I was hungry. More feedback was better.

And so, my blog was born. I started sharing my posts on Twitter and Facebook. My educator friends, personal friends, and family were reading, commenting, and asking me questions about my work. Every interaction that came from those posts gave me new perspectives and new ideas on how teaching and learning could look in my classroom.

As I shared and perused Twitter, I noticed Twitter chats—moderated conversations among groups that use a hashtag to follow one another—and I was hooked. I was part of live conversations with teachers from all over the world. We talked about project-based learning, effective technology integration, and a lot more.

Some of my fellow connected educators and I read one another's work and talked regularly. A few of us talked so often we planned in-person meetups at conferences. I've even co-presented with a couple of them. In one case we had never met in person before the day we presented together!

I can happily say that I no longer wait for professional development opportunities to come my way. When they do, it is great. But, when I'm ready to remix a project and bring new perspective to a topic, I have a whole network of people and resources at my fingertips.

Hands-On Learning

Traditional "sit and get" professional development no longer meets the mark. The days of teachers marching into a lecture hall, auditorium, or cafeteria to listen to a presenter for three hours is not scalable, affordable, or effective. Teachers should be actively engaged in the learning process. An easy way to achieve this is through "tinkering" style sessions where teachers are given times to discover and play with new technology tools in groups or independently. Teachers can also practice facilitating a blended learning lesson with other teachers playing the role of the students. This increases best practices sharing and collective innovation. These learner-driven approaches generate excitement, deeper learning, and multiple opportunities for "aha" moments. Another great approach to engage teachers more actively in professional learning is through gamification, or incorporating gaming elements, such as points, competition, badges, and so forth into learning. The Redbird Professional Learning Platform is an example of gamified professional development as teachers obtain points and badges for completion of projects and activities, and compete to raise their standing on the leaderboard. These types of approaches help to increase the fun of professional development while giving teachers a glimpse into the "gamer" world of many of their students.

Ongoing Learning

Schools must have a structure and environment of continued learning. The role of the leader should be to build this environment and structure. This structure should be ongoing and consistent. It should be a regular part of the week and possibly even the day. Sustainability is achieved when the community becomes a true learning community across all levels. School leadership, teachers, staff, and students should all view themselves as continuous learners. In a world of competing priorities, professional learning is often viewed as important, but not urgent. This is a real danger. When teachers are confronted with their daily schedule and numerous competing priorities, professional learning tends to take a back seat. The commitment must be made by the whole community to prioritize professional learning. This means making the space and time available for teachers to continue their learning.

Building the Structure of Continuous Learning at William Tilden Middle School, Philadelphia, Pennsylvania

Brian Johnson, Principal of Tilden Middle School, is determined to transform his school into the model blended learning school in Philadelphia. And he is on his way. First, Brian has established himself as the chief learner of his school. He takes advantage of every possible opportunity to get smart by attending conferences, connecting with other leaders across the country, and devouring articles and books on school transformation and blended learning. He recognizes that he is also modeling and setting the stage for his leadership team, teachers, and students. Brian is immersing his teachers in the same sort of learning that they should be replicate for their students. Professional development is inquiry-based and often delivered in station rotation models. He took the same risks with the teachers that they are taking in their classrooms with students and brought them into his planning and iteration process. They witnessed some of the challenges and mistakes he made in the transition process.

Brian is using tools like the Redbird Professional Learning Platform to augment the learning process for staff where they can drive more of their own development in synchronous and asynchronous ways. This is a 3-year growth sequence for the teachers and team at Tilden Middle. Over the course of this time, teachers will have their own personalized professional development paths as these professional learning supports are embedded into the fabric of the school. Brian sought advice from a professional scheduler to help him rethink the school day. He has found the time for teachers to have structured professional development three times per week after school. On Tuesday, they focus on social emotional learning, on Wednesday, blended learning or another focused topic, and Thursday, data review and academic growth. One of Brian's teachers has already decided to leap ahead and begin new courses in the professional learning platform on GAFE (Google Apps for Education) and Project-based learning. "This is the beauty of personalized learning," Brian says, "people have the opportunity of autonomy, to build new things, work at their pace, and create."

Mindset Shifts: Start With the Why Not the What

Often professional development for teachers launches immediately into a new skill, practice, or product without first addressing why it is important or explaining the purpose behind it. This approach undermines the importance of the learner actually being engaged in the process. If a teacher is not clear about the *why* of blended learning, it will be much more difficult to create the desire or willingness to actually try the practice in the classroom. Simon Sinek's research points to the effectiveness of inspired organizations in clearly communicating their purpose and mission (Sinek, 2009). The "why" is least effective when it is a top-down mandate or tied to punitive measures. It is most effective when teachers actually see the value in how this instructional practice will have a benefit in the classroom and to the learners. This can be achieved through leveraging current blended learning champions and leaders in the school in teacher-led sessions, coaching, and peer-to-peer classroom visits and observations. If the school does not currently have good models of blended learning, it may be a good idea to send teachers out to conferences or other schools to see and learn about the benefits. Lastly, even just starting professional learning sessions with a conversation and discussion of the "why" is of tremendous value.

Personalize Choice, Differentiation, Pace, and Skills

It is critical that professional learning experiences acknowledge that teachers are at different starting points, have different needs, and learn different ways. If a professional learning experience does not allow for this personalization, it is failing in two ways: 1) it is not providing teachers what they need to build their blended practice, and 2) it is not modeling for teachers how they should be rethinking their own classrooms for their students. There are a number of ways in which professional learning can be personalized, and not surprisingly they resemble how learning can be personalized for students: by pace, path, place, and modality. Later in this chapter, we discuss in much greater detail how schools and districts can differentiate professional development for different types of teachers.

LINKS TO THE CLASSROOM: WHAT ARE YOUR STRENGTHS NOW?

In new initiatives it is sometimes easy to feel that everything must change and fast. Be careful with this feeling as there are many practices that you are currently implementing that are working very well. Identify some of these strong practices, even taking the time to ask students what they currently love about the classroom learning experiences. In some cases, teachers may strategically decide not to change something dear to students, and in other cases to build it out through blended practices. This method of starting with strengths also increases the sustainability of the initiative.

Guiding Principle of Blended Learning Professional Development #2: Differentiate to Cross the Chasm

As you walk through the halls of most schools, one thing becomes immediately evident. A few classrooms have adopted blended learning practices and are zooming with technology integration while other classrooms (usually the majority) remain lecture oriented and more teacher-centered. This is the chasm. *The Tipping Point* by Malcolm Gladwell (2006) refers to the point at which an idea, concept, technology, or tool extends from being niche to part of the mainstream culture. In almost every adoption of new technology—from the new iPhone to the hoverboard—there is a progression of adoption. The bell curve pictured in Figure 4.2 largely holds true for the adoption of blended learning in schools. In most schools today, each of these groups of teachers exists. The chasm that we refer to is the divide between the early adopters and mainstream teachers.

FIGURE 4.2 The Technology Adoption Cycle

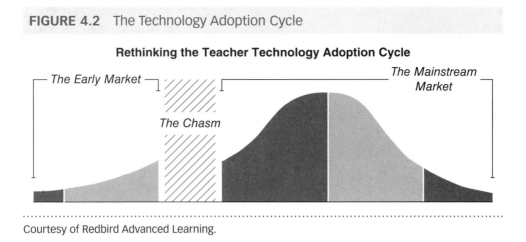

Courtesy of Redbird Advanced Learning.

Bridging the Gap/The Tipping Point

It is vital for schools to think about widespread transformation. In order to do this, we have to bridge the chasm to include adoption of the pragmatists and the conservatives. Take for example the wearable technology Google Glass. There was a small subset of people who jumped on board immediately. These are the tech enthusiasts and visionaries. They are willing to take risks with new models, products, and approaches. Many of them found value in being able to search news items right from their eyewear, get directions on the go, and maintain constant contact with information that's only a blink away. The challenge with Google Glass was that it never spread to reach the pragmatists and conservatives. The benefit never became clear, affordable, and usable enough for the mainstream, so Google Glass has largely faded out.

By contrast, when smartphones were first introduced, many people wondered why they would need a computer in their pocket; now nearly everyone who can afford a smartphone has one. Pragmatists adopted smartphones when they realized the added benefit in being able to pull directions, or easily check in online for a flight. Conservatives adopted smartphones when flip phones were no longer available or when they could no longer find the proper accessories. Eventually virtually everyone adopted the smartphone, but at different times and for different reasons.

This progression also holds true as it relates to blended learning adoption in schools. There are usually a few teachers in each school who are the tech enthusiasts and visionaries. They will try new technology tools and attempt to implement blended learning regardless of what the school does. Catlin Tucker's school was not doing any blended learning or tech integration, but she chose to make it work in her own low-tech classroom. She would be considered a visionary. There are many teachers like her who are pushing to make this transition regardless of what is happening in their school.

FIGURE 4.3 Differentiated Approaches to Professional Development

	TECHNOLOGY ENTHUSIASTS	VISIONARIES	CHASM	PRAGMATISTS	CONSERVATIVES	SKEPTICS
Current Practice	**FACILITATE** Using technology daily	**FACILITATE** Using technology daily		**LECTURE/ COORDINATE** Using technology 2–3x/wk	**LECTURE** Using technology 1–2x/wk	**LECTURE** Never use technology
SAMR Levels Achieved	*Redefinition*	*Modification & Redefinition*		*Substitution & Augmentation*	*Substitution*	*None*
Mindset and Receptivity	How can I connect my students with the world of learning and global peers through innovative practices and tools?	I love exploring new tools to enhance student learning. How can I build my practice to create more personalized learning paths?	Most schools have a handful of Tech Enthusiasts and Visionaries that have embraced the shift in learning. The chasm represents the divide between these early adopters and the mainstream of teachers.	I will do what makes instruction better especially if it makes me more efficient, but I'm not sure where to start or how to really benefit my students.	I don't understand how tech adds value to learning. I'll use it where I can but I'd rather do what I know works.	This is just the latest trend in education reform. It will pass.
Personalize Professional Development	**LET THEM FLY.** Provide freedom and time to find and tinker with new tools. Encourage participation in a PLN and conference presentations.	**GIVE CHOICE.** Provide resources to explore and grow at their own pace. Encourage PLN development and participation as a connected educator.	For true transformation, schools must strategically engage and support unique teacher needs with targeted approaches, expectations, and structures.	**GUIDE AND SUPPORT.** Develop a structured, incremental plan with a focus on practical application and quick wins. Provide 2–3 simple tech tools.	**ENGAGE AND DIRECT.** Focus first on mindset and the why of tech in classrooms. Provide 1 simple tech tool.	**CONVINCE.** Focus on mindset and creating greater openness. Have them observe blended classrooms.
Optimize Group	Capture learnings and best practices. Have them teach other teachers. Share outside the school as thought leaders.	Capture learnings and best practices. Have them teach other teachers.		Pair them up with a tech enthusiast or visionary. Capture successes.	Pair them up with a tech enthusiast or visionary. Capture successes.	Demonstrate success in other classes and show positive results and momentum in the school.
Mitigate Challenges	Ensure tech is being used with purpose and that quality of instruction and teacher/student rapport remain at the forefront.	Ensure tech is being used with purpose and that quality of instruction and teacher/student rapport remain at the forefront.		Ensure teachers continue to expand and grow their practice beyond substitution.	Ensure teachers reach toward new practices and do not slip into old habits of instruction.	Ensure that potential negative attitudes do not spread to other teachers.

Courtesy of Redbird Advanced Learning.

The mainstream of teachers tend to be more pragmatic or conservative in their approach to blended learning. Pragmatists want to see the tangible benefit and how it will make their lives easier, make them more efficient, or allow them to better engage students. Pragmatists are waiting until it is easier to grade student papers and submit grades online using the new Learning Management System compared to doing these activities on paper. Conservatives are waiting until paper-based systems are no longer an option. These groups may be trying a few things here and there, but they are largely waiting for the tipping point. If a school leader or district is trying to achieve large scale reform, these later adopters must be converted and approached differently. The good news . . . now, we can leverage technology in professional development to make this possible.

Figure 4.3 dives into the different groups and how school and district leadership can think about differentiating professional development across key groups of teachers and engaging them in the school's overall learning process.

WRAPPING IT UP

Most schools seeking to transition to a more blended instructional model to some degree are experiencing a wide distribution of adoption among teachers. The most successful schools and districts recognize these distinctions among teacher groups and provide professional development opportunities accordingly. In the planning of professional development, we highly recommend that the starting point is holistic in nature with broad goals and vision for the teaching and learning that we want to occur in the classroom. This will vary from district to district and even from school to school; however, this vision will generate the roadmap necessary for the plan for professional development to emerge.

By reiterating the guiding principles of blended learning professional development—

- As the student, so the teacher: building professional development experiences that reflect the practices and tenets of a blended and 21st-century classroom; and

- Differentiating to cross the chasm: establishing opportunities for teachers to learn in more personalized forms;

—schools will integrate and create a community of learning and learners fostering sustaining practice, and a higher quality of teaching and learning, ultimately leading to achievement gains among students.

BOOK STUDY QUESTIONS

1. What is your school or district's broader vision for the teaching and learning experience you want to create?

2. What are the skills that will be required for teachers to achieve this vision in the classroom?

3. How will you create a range of professional development opportunities and paths to better differentiate and ultimately personalize professional development?

4. How will you facilitate teachers engaging actively in their own professional development?

5. How will you measure the success of your professional development initiatives?

PART 2

Blended Learning Toolbox

Tiffany Wycoff

INTRODUCTION

When I moved to New York City in 2010, I remained in my role as a school leader at Grandview Preparatory School in Boca Raton, Florida, spending one week of every month on site and the rest of the time in the cloud. As one of the earliest one-to-one laptop schools, Grandview had been practicing forms of blended learning since its opening in 1997. These included blended learning models discussed later in Part 3, such as Rotation and A La Carte, but there had never been a scenario where the teacher for a whole class within this brick-and-mortar school was teaching mainly online, nor had there been an administrator managing via connected technology. This was a new adventure for all stakeholders!

Even though I began with a solid foundation for blended practice, I learned many lessons along the way as I led and taught from my kitchen on Reade Street in New York. I quickly accumulated a variety of tools aimed at fostering collaboration, community, and creativity. And then, overloaded with a heavy toolbox, I learned an appreciation for a few core tools. I experienced the thrill of being tightly connected through anytime-anywhere learning, and the multifaceted ways I got to know my students via this connection. And then, exhausted by being "on" all the time, I learned to set healthy expectations and turn off my device sometimes. I learned that my students didn't know quite as much about using technology as I thought they did. And then, I learned that they could be the best troubleshooters and hackers when we got stuck.

Of course, my students also learned a ton. They learned they didn't know quite as much about using technology as they thought they did. Some of them learned they did not like online learning while others thrived in the new interactions. They developed important skills, such as how to organize their academic work, communicate and collaborate with people who were not in the same room, and set goals and pace themselves. They also learned that having a teacher who can run down and film Occupy Wall Street before government class is an excellent resource to employ!

As you embark on this blended learning journey, think strategically about the tools you and your students need, how to measure your progress, and how best to support your students in their new learning environments; it helps make the road ahead much smoother. In Part 2 of this book, we explore just this, focusing on which decisions are critical early on and which can be more iterative. We delve into Devices & Digital Tools, Digital Curriculum, Assessment Tools, and Student Onboarding & Support. Through this study, you become better prepared to avoid pitfalls. Nevertheless, it is an adventure in learning with its share of detours, so the key is to have a growth mindset and a great team.

CHAPTER 5

Devices and Digital Tools

I feel most creative when my ideas are heard. When I feel acknowledged, my creativity is limitless.

—Elaine Baez, 8th Grade

When a district shifts to a blended learning model, one of the first issues that school leaders must consider is the budget for purchasing devices, improving infrastructure, and investing in online tools and applications. There are a growing number of options available to districts with money to invest in hardware and applications.

This chapter

- explains the function of a productivity suite and identifies the factors school leaders should consider when exploring the selection of a productivity environment;

- emphasizes the importance of building a technology toolbox to teach technology fluency;

- explores the different "critical spaces" in a digital classroom compared to the traditional classroom;

- describes the different types of devices a district should consider when selecting the right device for their budget and their students' needs;

- outlines three basic funding models that districts can use to purchase devices;

- identifies the benefits and challenges associated with using mobile devices, tablets, Chromebooks, and laptops; and

- highlights applications and web tools that teachers can use to cultivate the skills necessary to success beyond high school.

As illustrated in the *Blended Learning Roadmap,* selection of devices and digital tools starts in Planning and Design in Phase 1: Foundations and carries into the pre-pilot and pilot phase.

 DIFFERENT TOOLS FOR A DIFFERENT GENERATION

As the educational landscape shifts and changes, the tools that teachers and students use both inside and outside of the classroom must also change. Although most teachers were taught with traditional tools—books, paper, pencils—students today are embracing a new set of tools for communicating, collaborating, sharing, and learning. It's crucial that educators, even those who do not consider themselves tech-savvy, build their own technology toolboxes. If teachers do not incorporate the tools students rely on outside of school into the classroom, students will find the work they do in school increasingly disconnected and irrelevant to their lives.

> If teachers do not incorporate the tools students rely on outside of school into the classroom, students will find the work they do in school increasingly disconnected and irrelevant to their lives. #BLinAction

Given the increasing ubiquity of devices among young people, teachers should incorporate these tools into the classroom to teach skills that students need to leverage their devices for learning. According to research conducted by the Pew Research Center in 2015, "73% of teens have a smartphone" (Anderson, 2015, para. 1), and "92% of teens report going online daily–with 24% using the internet 'almost constantly'" (Lenhart, 2015, p. 1). The growing number of teens with devices and access to the internet means that students have access to limitless amounts of information, applications, and online resources. When harnessed properly, these can be powerful tools for learning.

Forbes (Adams, 2014) identified the top skills employers wanted in 2015 graduates. At the top of the list were the ability to (1) "work in a team structure," (2) "make decisions and problem solve," (3) "communicate verbally," (4) "plan, organize, and prioritize work," and (5) "obtain and process information" (Adams, 2014, p. 1). Also on the list of the top ten skills employers want was "proficiency with computer software programs." Given how much work happens online today, students must learn how to use technology, work asynchronously with a team, communicate effectively online, and find digital resources to plan and problem solve. Often online skills are neglected in the traditional classroom; however, the importance of these skills is also reflected in the International Society for Technology in Education standards.

The 2016 ISTE Standards for Students provide a helpful guideline for the knowledge and skills students need to be successful in an increasingly global and digital society (ISTE, 2016). The ISTE Standards for Students (2016) identifies seven specific standards for students:

1. Empowered Learner

2. Digital Citizen

3. Knowledge Constructor

4. Innovative Designer

5. Computational Thinker

6. Creative Communicator

7. Global Collaborator

It's imperative that teachers actively teach students the skills they need to communicate, collaborate, and create using technology and the internet. However, the sheer number of devices, applications, and online resources can be daunting for a school shifting to a blended learning model.

 ## BUILDING BLOCKS OF A DIGITAL CLASSROOM

Just like a traditional classroom, the digital classroom has critical spaces where students access course materials and engage with each other. For example, students must have a consistent location where they can access information, such as a class agenda and homework. In the classroom, important information is written on a board for students to view and record. Similarly, the blended classroom must also have an online location where students can find important information. Teachers can post information to a website, class blog, homepage of an LMS (Learning Management System), or send text message reminders. Table 5.1 breaks down some of the critical spaces students need in both the traditional face-to-face classroom and online for a blended learning model to work effectively.

As teachers move from a traditional classroom to a blended learning model, they must be mindful of selecting technology tools that allow the flow of information, communication, collaboration, and creation to begin in one learning medium—in class or online—and extend seamlessly into the other. It is only when various learning mediums are woven together that the blended learning model is most effective.

Although much of the discussion about the technology integration is focused on the types of devices and costs to the schools, it is important to remember that the device is simply the vehicle we use to connect students to information and resources in order to cultivate specific skills they need to be successful in life.

LINKS TO LEADERSHIP: SUPPORTING AN ITERATIVE PRACTICE

As teachers are empowered to use various tools in their classrooms, it is important for school leaders to embrace "fail-forward" moments. Too often, school leaders become fearful of mistakes that students can make online using collaborative tools rather than embracing those teachable moments for students and teachers. Instead of shutting down the use of a tool after an incident of inappropriate interaction or misuse, school leaders should engage teachers and students in solutions that allow for the more responsible use of the tool. Through this practice, school leaders continue to build a positive, growth-oriented blended learning culture.

TABLE 5.1 Critical Spaces for Learning

CRITICAL LEARNING SPACES	TRADITIONAL CLASSROOM	DIGITAL CLASSROOM
Information	On the board	Website Blog Homepage of an LMS Text message reminders Calendar
Discussion	Whole group and small group real-time conversations	Asynchronous discussions e.g., Schoology Video conferencing (e.g., Google Hangouts or Skype) Communication Apps (e.g., VoiceThread or Voxer) Sharing Apps (e.g., Twitter, Today's Meet, or Padlet)
Collaboration	Small group work at desks	Google Apps Microsoft Office 364
Creation	Limited to tools and supplies in the classroom: • Pens • Paper • Glue • Rulers	Limitless online applications, Chrome extensions, and web tools to create: • Presentations • Videos • Artwork • Storybooks • Infographics • Websites

Productivity and Collaboration Environments

In October 2006, Google launched Google Apps for Education (GAFE), a free cloud-based productivity suite with tools comparable to the Microsoft

Office suite. This offering is enticing for schools from a financial perspective as the migration to GAFE results in significant savings in both licensing and server maintenance expenses. GAFE also gives teachers and students a chance to collaborate in the same shared documents, which can be accessed by multiple users with internet access. Google for Education has grown to over twenty-five million users worldwide and has become an industry standard for collaborative cloud applications.

Teachers in blended learning classrooms can use Google for Education tools to blend work done in class with work done online as pictured in Table 5.2.

GAFE is no longer the only open-source productivity solution that schools can implement on a district or schoolwide basis. In 2012, Microsoft released Office 365 Education which offers a free version to schools of its Office 365 for Business. Similar to GAFE, Office 365 is cloud-based and offers comparable productivity tools. Unlike GAFE, Office 365 is a freemium model which offers more services for enterprise, fee-based integration. (Freemium is a pricing strategy by which a product or service—typically a digital offering or application, such as software, media, games, or web services—provided free of charge, but money or a premium is charged for proprietary features, functionality, or virtual goods.)

As more learning applications and devices have hit the market, the integration of systems has become more essential so that all the systems communicate

TABLE 5.2 Google for Education: Applications and Uses in a Blended Classroom

TOOLS	BLENDED LEARNING APPLICATION
Classroom	• Assign work, collect, and grade digital work • Post class announcements and engage students in discussion • Manage Google Drive activity for each class
Drive	• Organize files in shared folders • Build student portfolios • Collaborate on curriculum and faculty resource collections
Documents "Google Docs"	• Collaborate on written assignments and projects • Provide teacher feedback and editing through comments and "suggesting" mode with Documents • Design collaborative multimedia presentations using Slides • Explore data, charts, and information management through Sheets • Survey students and document progress easier with Forms
Email	• Communicate with students • Facilitate peer communication • Teach digital citizenship and communication standards
Calendar	• Help students manage their schedules • Post homework assignments or class events to shared Calendar
Blogger	• Engage students in class or individual blogging • Connect with other classes to form learning communities

properly with one another. Many learning applications are now integrated with GAFE or Office 365 so that students can create their accounts and log in via a "single sign-on," meaning they sign-on with their GAFE or Office 365 credentials. Further, each environment has additional tools, including many learning applications, which can be added to a user's dashboard. Because of this integration and supplemental application marketplaces, it is important for school and district leaders to carefully consider the selection of the productivity environment early on in the *Blended Learning Roadmap;* not doing so can lead to complications down the road. For example, a school selecting Chromebooks as a device would find a higher level of integration with a GAFE environment than a Microsoft one.

Learning Management Systems

Unlike a productivity environment where teachers and students actually do their work, the learning management system (LMS) is a space where work and ideas are shared. An LMS

> is a software application or web-based technology used to plan, implement, and assess a specific learning process. Typically, a learning management system provides an instructor with a way to create and deliver content, monitor student participation, and assess student performance. (Rouse, 2016, p. 1)

An LMS has the advantage of offering a wide range of features and functionality in a single place with a single sign-on.

Many schools adopt an LMS early in their transition to a blended learning model as a strategy to get all of the teachers on one campus or in a single district on the same page in terms of technology. For schools and districts, the selection and implementation of an LMS is an easy place to start because it provides teachers a place to house, organize, and disseminate information related to their courses. The LMS is found in Phase 2: Transitions in the *Blended Learning Roadmap* to give an opportunity for a small group of teachers to pilot before a full-scale rollout.

Teachers can use an LMS to create individual courses, post assignments, engage students in asynchronous discussions, administer tests and quizzes, and track student progress.

This convenience is incredibly attractive given that most schools and districts transitioning to a blended learning model are wrestling with the logistical challenges of getting a large number of teachers and an even greater number of students online successfully. Consistency and ease of use are often paramount concerns for leaders who want to make integrating tech as painless as possible—especially for members of the school community who have resisted the move to integrated online learning into the traditional classroom.

The cost of an LMS is a primary factor in the selection process, so district leaders must identify a clear budget before exploring the LMS market. Once a budget has been established, leaders should identify the features and functionality that are important to teachers. Ideally, teachers should have an opportunity to "test drive" more than one LMS to see which ones are most user-friendly and provide the functionality that is most important to them. Since several LMS platforms operate with a freemium business model, schools can proceed through the pre-pilot and pilot phases using mainly individual teacher accounts, keeping in mind the extra features that come with an enterprise fee-based integration.

LINKS TO LEADERSHIP: ACCESS TO TECHNOLOGY

Leaders must make decisions about large scale purchases, like the purchase of a learning management system (LMS). Here are some questions to consider.

- What is the school or district budget for purchasing technology hardware versus applications?

- What are the benefits of investing in a single LMS for all teachers as opposed to allowing teachers to select and independently use a free LMS? What added features, support, and/or functionality of the LMS come with a school or district purchase?

- Who will take the lead in researching LMS options? Will this person compile a "short list" of LMS options for the school or district to consider?

Decisions and purchases should be part of the larger conversation among stakeholders about the tools needed to shift to a blended learning model. Teachers are more likely to use a learning management system if they've participated in the conversation about **why** purchasing an LMS will help them to more effectively shift to a blended learning model, and which features are necessary to engage students in work related to their curriculum.

- How will you engage teachers in a conversation about the features and functionality they want in an LMS?

- Will there be time set aside for teachers to explore LMS options?

- What method will you use to survey your staff to compile data about their preferences?

(Continued)

(Continued)

LINKS TO LEADERSHIP: PROFESSIONAL DEVELOPMENT

Once an LMS is selected, teachers need to be trained how to use it. Because each LMS has many different and distinct features, at first it can be challenging for a teacher to navigate. Professional development can be handled in a few different ways.

- Schools and districts paying for an LMS may receive training from the LMS company—depending on the contract. This training may be online via on-demand webinars or in-person. If they are on-demand webinars, leaders should build time into the schedule for teachers to watch the webinars and explore the tools together. The best strategy for this type of training is to group teachers with colleagues who teach their same subject and/or grade level and focus on one feature of the LMS at a time. A series of short trainings that encourage teachers to play with a single feature and then return to their classroom to try that feature with students is more effective than a lengthy training that attempts to cover every aspect of the LMS in one sitting.

- If the LMS company sends a trainer to deliver professional development, it's important to complement that with "playtime" sessions where teachers are encouraged to experiment with different features while surrounded by colleagues with whom they can have conversations and troubleshoot.

Schoology, an LMS or course management system, published a resource titled "7 Best Practices for Getting Faculty Buy-in for a New LMS" (2016) that identifies the following tips for getting teachers to adopt and consistently use an LMS:

1. Communicate with teachers before, during, after, and often

2. Provide iterative training, not a single training event

3. Use your LMS to deliver professional development to model the value of your LMS for learning

4. Focus on ease of use

5. Support your early adopters

6. Embed your LMS in your institutional culture

7. Emphasize how the LMS will improve student learning

These best practices help make the adoption and use of an LMS more successful.

Although the learning management systems attempt to offer one-stop shopping in terms of technology needs, it's important that teachers also explore stand-alone apps and tools.

Just as there isn't one tool in life that solves every problem, though the Swiss Army Knife valiantly attempted this feat, there is no one piece of technology or software that solves every problem. The reality is that certain tools work well for particular tasks. It's important for teachers and students to understand this if we are to move students from technology literacy to technology fluency.

> Certain tools work well for particular tasks. #BLinAction

Building Technology Toolboxes to Promote Technology Fluency

Technology literate students know what to do with technology and how to use it competently to accomplish a task. Fluency requires more experience and expertise. Students who are technology fluent know *when* to use a tool, and *why* the tool they are using is the best tool for a specific job. Beyond simply using technology competently, fluency requires that students demonstrate a high degree of skill or proficiency when selecting and employing technology.

It is easier to move students from literacy to fluency if they are exposed to many different types of technology tools during their time in school. If students are encouraged to use a range of tools to complete a variety of tasks, they begin to appreciate that different tools do different jobs well. Then when they approach a novel situation, they are more likely to select the best piece of technology for that specific situation or task from a range of tools. Because apps and tools change, it's also crucial that students develop flexibility when it comes to using technology. If students are only exposed to a single LMS or technology tool, they will struggle to solve problems if that particular tool is no longer available.

If a school or district decides to purchase and use a learning management system, teachers should still be encouraged to build their own technology toolbox composed of a collection of apps and online resources. Although some teachers balk at the need to create various accounts and remember multiple log-ins and passwords, often applications and online web tools can be integrated into an LMS for convenience or accessed using the single sign-on process.

Deciding on the Right Device

In U.S. Secretary of Education Arne Duncan's "Future Ready Schools: Building Technology Infrastructure for Learning" (2014), he accurately states that "the educational benefits of increased connectivity are realized only when internet enabled devices are available to teachers and students" (Duncan, 2014, p. 44). When faced with a potential purchase, the report suggests schools create a "testing script," or a list of tasks teachers and students should try on each device. For example, when compiling the list for a testing script, schools should prioritize the types of functions they want teachers and students to execute with technology. If video creation is a priority, then devices must have the necessary functionality to record, edit, and publish videos.

> Technology literate students know what to do with technology and how to use it competently to accomplish a task. #BLinAction

In addition to functionality, schools should consider all of the costs associated with purchasing a particular device because some devices require additional equipment, such as keyboards or protective cases. All of these peripheral expenses should be considered as those costs can be significant.

Duncan's report encourages schools to consider the following questions when deciding which devices are right for their schools:

- What are your expectations for extended battery life?

- How reliable is the device's operating system relative to privacy and data storage concerns, and does this align with your district's privacy policy?

- What level of durability are you looking for in the device(s)?

- To what extent are considerations of screen size, keyboard/mouse, and peripherals like scientific probes important for device selection?

- Given the ages of the students who will be using these devices, what choices are most developmentally appropriate? (Duncan, 2014, p. 46)

Additionally, as previously mentioned, the integration of the device with the productivity environment, LMS, and learning applications is also an important consideration. Even though each type of device is compatible with a different set of applications and online tools, they can **all** be used to develop the skills identified by Forbes and ISTE as keys to success in life beyond school.

Which Funding Model Is the Best Fit?

If your district decides to purchase devices, schools can keep costs low by being mindful of how they develop their purchasing agreements. The Office of Education Technology suggests

Issuing a request for proposal (RFP) instead of requesting a price quote makes vendors compete for your business, leading to more competitive prices for your district. For small districts that may not be requesting large enough proposals to attract bids, partnering with other districts or states on collaborative purchases is a good option. (Duncan, 2014, p. 48)

There are three funding models that schools and districts should consider: outright purchase, lease, and cooperative purchases. Table 5.3 explains each type of funding model.

The funding model a district selects will largely depend on its financial situation. Establishing a budget for purchases is the first step. Then exploring the short-term and long-term costs associated with each model will make it clear which one is the best fit for your district.

TABLE 5.3 Funding Models for Purchasing Devices

Outright Purchase	The district buys and owns the devices purchased. This approach requires that the district allocate annual funding to maintain and update these devices. Because technology changes so rapidly, the outright purchase of devices may result in students using outdated technology.
Lease	The leasing company owns the devices and the districts use them for a specific period of time in exchange for payment. Depending on the terms of the lease agreement, the company may be responsible for maintaining and updating devices.
Cooperative Purchase	In this model, districts purchase devices from "regional, state, or consortium-based purchasing contracts. These contracts can offer volume-purchase and discount pricing for smaller or medium-size school districts". (Duncan, 2014, p. 49)

Mobile Devices

Many schools shifting to a blended learning model cannot afford to invest in both hardware and infrastructure. This should not be a barrier to adopting a blended learning model, but does require that districts and schools embrace a "bring your own device" (BYOD) policy to capitalize on student-owned devices. An increasing number of schools are encouraging students to bring their own devices, so they can invest the money they have in improving infrastructure to support those devices. According to the Digital School Districts Survey conducted by the Center for Digital Education and National School Boards Association, the percentage of BYOD schools increased from twenty-two to fifty-six percent in 2014 (Schaffhauser, 2014, p. 1).

There are several benefits and drawbacks to a BYOD model that capitalizes on student devices. The financial benefits of this model are obvious. It's an expensive proposition to purchase a device for every student and keep up with the maintenance of that hardware. If students are responsible for bringing their own devices, then money can be invested into improving infrastructure. Table 5.4 identifies some of the key benefits and challenges of a BYOD policy that relies primarily on smartphones.

TABLE 5.4 Benefits and Challenges of Adopting a BYOD Policy With Mobile Devices

BENEFITS	CHALLENGES
Using student owned devices saves the district money on hardware.	Not all families can afford to purchase a device. This creates barriers to learning for economically disadvantaged students who may not be able to easily access information or course materials online. **Solution:** Purchase devices and set up a lease program for those students without personal devices.
Students are more comfortable working on their own devices. These are the devices they navigate the world with and using them in class teaches them how to leverage them for learning.	The variety of devices can create challenges for teachers as they plan and facilitate a lesson. Some devices may be incompatible with the online activities. Other students may need help troubleshooting a problem with a device that is unfamiliar to the teacher. **Solution:** Teachers should make a habit of testing out lesson activities on their personal devices prior to each lesson, encourage collaboration if there is a compatibility issue, and use students as tech support in the classroom.
Because the devices go home with the students, it encourages students to continue learning after they've left the classroom.	Security can be an issue, especially if teachers are using devices for assessment. **Solution:** Design assessments that do not rely on technology or schedule time in a computer lab for online assessments.

Tablets

There are a variety of tablets available on the market–iPad, Lenovo, and Google Nexus. Tablets were an early favorite for districts, particularly at the elementary level, with many making large purchases. Despite being the most widely purchased tablets for schools, iPad sales for education fell in 2014 to 2.7 million, down from 2.9 million in 2013 (Singer, 2015). This decrease may be a result of the increasing popularity of the relatively low cost of Chromebooks, which have seen significant growth in the education market.

Tablets have several benefits and drawbacks. Table 5.5 identifies some of the key benefits and challenges associated with purchasing tablets for a 1:1 initiative or for mobile carts.

It's important to note the first two solutions proposed in Table 5.5 require that the district purchase additional equipment that will drive up the total cost of purchasing tablets. These are the peripheral costs districts must consider before making a purchase.

TABLE 5.5 Benefits and Challenges of Purchasing Tablets

BENEFITS	CHALLENGES
Tablets are lightweight and tend to have a long battery life.	The screens can be damaged, especially if students are carrying them around in their backpacks. **Solution:** The district can order protective cases to protect the screens.
The touch screen interface is ideal for young learners who do not have keyboarding skills.	The touch screen is not ideal for older students using the devices to type lengthy pieces of writing. This may also make it challenging for students to complete digital standardized assessments that require significant typing. **Solution:** The district can order Bluetooth keyboards.
Tablets are compatible with a range of applications that offer teachers working at various grade levels and subject areas access to specific apps ideal for their individual classes.	Web-based applications may not be optimized for use on a tablet, limiting the online tools teachers can use with students. **Solution:** Use the browser on the tablet to access web-based applications.
There are numerous learning applications, spanning every grade and subject, available for integration via tablets.	The management of application installation can be tedious and complicated, especially for those requiring purchase in bulk. **Solution:** Appoint a central individual for managing this process and protocol for teachers to request App installation.
The learning applications are frequently built for one user, offering a level of personalization through an adaptive interface.	The single user setup of most applications makes sharing of tablets difficult to manage. **Solution:** Class sets are much more suited to tablet integration.

Chromebooks

Chromebooks are computers that run using Google's Chrome operating system. A new report from Futuresource Consulting found that "Chromebook sales now account for more than half of all devices sold for U.S. classrooms, up from less than 1 percent in 2012" (Taylor, 2015, p. 1). In 2014, "3.9 million Chromebooks were shipped in the education sector, an increase . . . of more than 310 percent compared to 2013" (Singer, 2015, para. 9). With an increasing number of schools with Google for Education accounts, Chromebooks are increasingly popular. They are more affordable than tablets, laptops, or desktop computers, which is a bonus for districts on a budget. Unlike the aforementioned tools, Chromebooks do not offer storage space, so it's crucial that students use Google Drive to save their documents, presentations, and other online work to the cloud. For more, see Table 5.6.

Students using Chromebooks can add functionality to their Chrome browser with Chrome Extensions. Chrome Extensions are "small software programs that can modify and enhance the functionality of the Chrome browser" (Chrome, n.d.). Because Chrome Extensions bundle multiple files into a single file that the user downloads and installs, they do not rely on content from the web in order to work. This makes them different from web applications that depend on online content to operate. Chrome Extensions and settings for these devices can be managed at the group level using Google's Chromebook Management Console. This makes device and application management significantly easier, but does add costs to consider.

TABLE 5.6 Benefits and Challenges of Purchasing Chromebooks

BENEFITS	CHALLENGES
Chromebooks are more affordable than traditional laptops.	Limited hard drive/offline storage can be an obstacle for students who are not using cloud-based programs. **Solution:** Students can use a cloud-based productivity environment, like Google Apps, that do not require them to save anything to their devices.
Chromebooks connect students with a ton of free apps that add functionality to their browser for integration via Chrome Web Store.	Chromebooks must be connected to Wi-Fi to work. **Solution:** Use money saved investing in Chromebooks, as opposed to more expensive devices, to invest in boosting the internet infrastructure.
Chromebooks have management software that allows the school to easily add applications and control settings.	Some models can wear and break easily. **Solution:** Research different models to find Chromebooks that receive high ratings for durability. Implement "norms" for transporting and storing Chromebooks on campus.

Laptops

Laptops were the first real mobile option when it came to computers. However, the last decade has introduced a wide range of devices that are more mobile than the traditional laptop. That said, laptops are still an option for schools looking to put devices with robust functionality, storage space, and longer battery lives into the hands of students.

There may also be a strong case made for purchasing laptops at the secondary level because trends at the college level reveal that laptops are the mobile device of choice for college students. In a recent Harris Poll, eighty-seven percent of college students still prefer their laptops to tablets or smartphones for work. And almost half of all college students surveyed said they "preferred laptops most of all mobile devices" (Harris Poll, 2015). Chromebooks are included in this number, but many college courses still require work submitted in more traditional formats like Word, as opposed to Google documents.

Table 5.7 identifies a few of the benefits and challenges of purchasing laptops for students. Note that the solution proposed to address the first challenge requires additional funding to purchase and install charging stations in classrooms.

TABLE 5.7 Benefits and Challenges of Purchasing Laptops

BENEFITS	CHALLENGES
Unlike tablets, laptops have larger screens, built in keyboards, and more storage than Chromebooks.	The battery life of a laptop may not be as robust as that of a tablet. **Solution:** Set up charging stations in classrooms so students can charge laptops throughout the day.
Advanced software can be installed on laptops to allow students to create their own media.	Laptops are more expensive than most tablets and Chromebooks. **Solution:** Districts can opt for the lease funding model to cut down on the cost of laptops.

Laptops come with software programs installed that can be used for learning. PC laptops typically come with the Microsoft Office suite of tools, including Word, PowerPoint, and Excel. Mac laptops come with their own software: Pages, Numbers, Keynote, and iMovie. The software packages that come with laptops are also attractive to many schools that may not be using Google Apps for Education or cloud-based applications.

Finding the Right Tool

Apps and technology tools are constantly changing. Some disappear just as we are mastering them, while others continually change as the company iterates and improves on the technology. It's important that teachers know where to find apps and edtech (educational technology) tools. Common Sense Education (www.commonsense.org/education/) and Edsurge Index (www.edsurge.com) provide reviews and ratings for educators looking for specific technology tools.

These resources incorporate search functionality and filters so that teachers at different grade levels and in different subject areas can find tools perfect for their students. Teachers can filter by the type of tool they are looking for (apps, console and PC games, and websites), device compatibility, subject area, grade level, price, skills, and purpose. Results include a brief description, ratings, and reviews. These are fabulous tools for keeping up with all the new technology offerings in the education space.

Stay Connected and Keep Learning

As noted, Common Sense Education and Edsurge Index are two tools teachers can use to find highly rated technology that is ideal for their subject area and grade level, but there are other avenues teachers can use to stay current on technology offerings. Most teachers who have embraced technology have also embraced the power of social media to continue learning. Connecting with and learning from other inspiring educators is the best way to stay excited about the potential of engaging students with technology.

> Connecting with and learning from other inspiring educators is the best way to stay excited about the potential of engaging students with technology. #BLinAction

It doesn't matter where teachers go to connect—Twitter, Pinterest, Periscope, or Facebook. What is more important is finding a space where they are comfortable connecting and sharing with other educators.

Leaders in a school community can model the importance of using social media to connect, share, and learn. Principals can write a blog about what's new on their campus; schools can set up a Twitter handle and post videos of events on YouTube. If teachers see that school leaders are using these tools, they'll be more likely to use them as well.

WRAPPING IT UP

A district or school moving from a traditional teaching model to a blended learning model must make important decisions about devices and technology tools. Although many districts begin by purchasing a large learning management system that offers lots of functionality in one location, it's important to encourage teachers to build their own technology toolbox that they can use in their practice. The more tools that students are able to use to communicate, collaborate, research, problem solve, create, and innovate, the more likely the student will graduate school technologically fluent.

In order to develop that technological fluency and learn how to use technology, teachers and students must have access to devices and the internet. Deciding which device is best for a district or school can be a challenging task. It's important to consider everything from the cost to functionality.

Each device works well with particular software, applications, and web tools. Using tools like Common Sense Education and connecting with other educators on social media helps keep teachers informed about new technology tools that enter the education space. The tools constantly change, but new ones pop up to take their places. This constant flux requires that educators be flexible and continue to learn.

BOOK STUDY QUESTIONS

1. Do you and other teachers in your school have experience using Google for Education or Office 365? What is the most natural fit for your community? Explore the pros and cons of each within the context of your setting.

2. Do you plan to use a Learning Management System? If so, what factors are most important as you explore the LMS market? How will you ensure that all stakeholders are involved in the conversation about which features are most important in an LMS?

3. How can using multiple tools help to develop technology fluency? What challenges does using multiple tools present for both district and school leaders as well as teachers? How can these challenges be addressed so they do not limit learning?

4. Think about the critical spaces identified in this chapter. What would you add to this list? How will you set up these critical spaces in your classroom and online? What tools will you need to use to create them online?

5. Given the information presented on the various devices available, which do you think your district is most likely to purchase? Are there peripheral costs you need to consider? Is your infrastructure capable of supporting the devices you've selected? What funding model will you use?

6. As several applications, Chrome Extensions, and web tools were highlighted in this chapter, what technology tools would you add to your list of go-to tools? Considering the ISTE Standards for Students, which skills do those tools target?

CHAPTER 6

Digital Curriculum

I feel most creative when the topic of the assignment is not narrowed down to the point where everyone is doing the same work.

—Angel Cruz, 9th Grade

WHAT IS DIGITAL CURRICULUM?

Teachers and students have access to a wide landscape of digital tools and curriculum. To visualize how these resources fit in the classroom planning process, it is helpful to distinguish digital curriculum from other digital apps and tools. Digital curriculum is composed of tools that come with instructional content that could replace the delivery of a lesson.

Other apps and tools like those covered in Chapter 5 can be transformative and extend learning, but do not include prepopulated instructional content. Digital curriculum can be a simple entry point for modifying lesson delivery in a blended learning classroom as teachers can replace existing offline resources with adaptive, multimedia curriculum. As teachers become more skilled in integrating tools beyond digital curriculum, they can move from basic substitution levels of technology integration to truly redefining learning.

As illustrated in the *Blended Learning Roadmap,* we recommend a gradual integration of digital curriculum starting with a pre-pilot and pilot in Phase 1: Foundations, transitioning to supplemental use in Phase 2: Transitions, and then expanding into core usage in Phase 3: Expansion.

Types of Digital Curriculum

It is helpful to think about digital curriculum in these four categories:

1. **Core Textbook Replacement.** These are digital curriculum tools which could take the place of whole traditional textbooks. Students and teachers can use these tools on a daily or regular basis in a given course.

2. **Supplemental Textbook Replacement.** These are digital curriculum tools that can supplement a core traditional textbook. Students can

use these tools on an ongoing basis for targeted interventions, remediation, or acceleration.

3. **Lecture Replacement.** These are digital curriculum tools that can replace a direct instruction lecture or lesson. A teacher can identify or create a specific video to use in place of delivering an in-class lecture.

4. **Workbook Replacement.** These are digital curriculum tools that take the place of workbooks, worksheets, or other practice activities. Students can use these tools for practice and application to reinforce a previously introduced skill or to learn a new skill in a learn-by-doing fashion.

What Are the Benefits of Digital Curriculum?

Digital curriculum enables teachers to plan effectively for differentiated and personalized instruction by reducing the amount of time needed to create instructional content to meet the needs of every learner.

There are few resources more valuable to a teacher than planning time. In the limited time outside of instructional hours, teachers must tend to lesson planning, meetings, parent communication, and grading. Differentiating instruction at a level of detail required to truly reach each student is a demanding and time-consuming task. Differentiation mandates teachers provide multiple resources, learning pathways, and outcomes for their students. This is where digital content can create more efficiency in lesson planning and grant teachers more time to focus on other elements of instructional preparation in a differentiated setting. As teachers begin to use powerful tools to deliver or supplement instruction via technology, they spend less time developing their own instructional content and more time building engaging learning experiences. Teachers can use the time gained to creatively design and support projects, review data, and complete targeted interventions.

FIGURE 6.1   Digital Curriculum Defined

CORE TEXTBOOK REPLACEMENT	SUPPLEMENTAL TEXT BOOK REPLACEMENT	LECTURE REPLACEMENT	WORKBOOK REPLACEMENT
• online book/ multimedia resource • complete scope and sequence • regularly used	• videos, articles • multiple resources from range of sites • used as needed for specific unit or learning target	• short videos or podcasts • made by teachers or curated by teachers for use in instruction • replaces a lecture or lesson	• practice site for skill-building • contains activities • used frequently to practice or learn a new skill

Figure 6.2 illustrates the way digital curriculum can be leveraged for efficiency in planning for differentiated instruction.

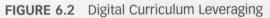

FIGURE 6.2   Digital Curriculum Leveraging

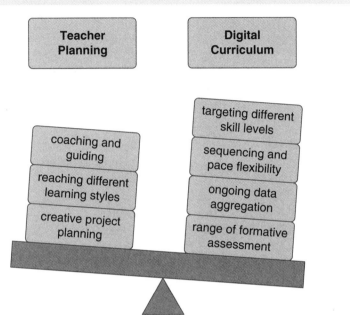

How Can Digital Curriculum Foster Student Ownership?

The next level of differentiated instruction—personalized learning—transitions from "teacher-as-driver" to "student-as-driver." As compared by Barbara Bray and Kathleen McClaskey in their *Personalization vs. Differentiation vs. Individualization Chart,* a key distinguisher of personalized learning is its "learner-driven" design. In personalized learning, students "drive their own learning," whereas in a differentiated setting, teachers "provide instruction to groups of learners" (Bray & McClaskey, 2014, p. 1). Through personalization, students become primary stakeholders in their learning. In a personalized learning environment, students are empowered to help design their learning experiences in partnership with their teachers who help them set learning goals, seek valuable resources, build pathways to learning, and create their learning outcomes. Whereas a differentiated instruction setting often caters to meet the needs of learners within small groups, as teachers move toward a more personalized learning model, the goal shifts from small group to individual learner differentiation. A personalized learning model significantly leverages digital curriculum so that teachers are able to provide multiple learning pathways for their students.

> In a personalized learning environment, students are empowered to help design their learning experiences in partnership with their teachers. #BLinAction

What Are the Challenges of Using Digital Curriculum?

In differentiating or personalizing instruction, teachers can benefit from digital curriculum, but should anticipate and plan for some challenges. The benefits and challenges of digital curriculum are outlined in Figure 6.3.

FIGURE 6.3 Benefits and Challenges of Digital Curriculum

BENEFITS	CHALLENGES
Provides a broader scope of instructional content so that teachers can effectively meet learning needs ranging from remediation to acceleration and enrichment.	The number of options makes it difficult for teachers to select valuable content with confidence. The task of curating the right digital curriculum can be time-consuming. **Solution:** set aside time for curating, and focus on a few core tools.
Engage students with different learning styles via multimedia and the often interactive nature of digital curriculum.	Even the best digital curriculum will fall flat if used as the sole instructional experience. **Solution:** balance use of digital curriculum with other learning experiences that are student-centered, hands-on, collaborative, and creative.
Allow for individualized pacing of instruction through adaptive technology.	Digital curriculum works differently across devices. **Solution:** it is important to select the appropriate curriculum to match the student devices and browsers.
Provides resources to match any student's interest in personalizing learning.	Anyone can post instructional content to open-source sites, compromising quality. **Solution:** teachers must review resources shared by other teachers for accuracy and quality.
Offer cost reductions via free digital curriculum or relatively less expensive subscription fees compared to textbook programs.	While there are several free options for digital curriculum, a comprehensive curriculum can be expensive, especially where the content is adaptive and provides rich data. **Solution:** Use a free version in the pre-pilot phase to gauge value and look to reallocate from other core resources like textbooks.
In a flipped class model, digital curriculum can be used to expose students to instruction at home and allow for in-class experiences to be more hands-on and engaging.	

How Do I Select the Right Digital Curriculum?

Just as there are standards for evaluating and selecting traditional curriculum resources, there are also standards for choosing the best digital curriculum; however, there are some important distinctions in the process of selection.

In a more traditional model, core curriculum providers are selected via department or committee. In a blended learning model, teachers have direct access to online curriculum providers and should be empowered to curate free resources best suited to their classrooms, and to make recommendations for department-level purchase of digital curriculum. In this model, both teachers and students can inform the selection of core resources based on firsthand experience with digital curriculum.

Figure 6.4 illustrates a student- and teacher-driven process for the selection of fee-based digital curriculum. In the pre-pilot phase, teacher trailblazers can try out digital content and obtain student feedback regarding the user experience and engagement level. This information then flows to a team of teachers to select a pilot group for premium access. The use of pilot programs within schools allows for committees and schools to thoroughly evaluate a resource before making a significant investment, and to form the best implementation plan for a more expansive use of it.

FIGURE 6.4   Selection Process for Digital Curriculum

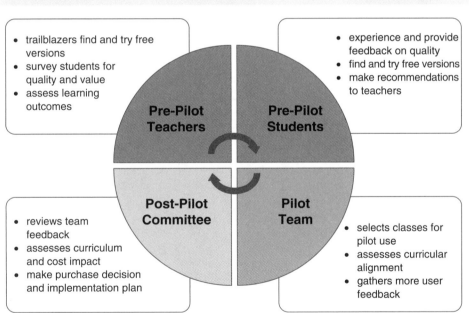

As part of the process of selecting digital curriculum, schools must evaluate each resource to determine its programmatic worth. This evaluation will be different for each school as teachers and administrators measure the benefits of a digital offering against the school's unique mission, pedagogy, student body, teacher culture, and scope and sequence. Teacher trailblazers and administrators can work together in developing a rubric for evaluating digital curriculum. The use of a rubric can then empower individual teachers to review and assess the value of an online resource. A sample template for such a rubric is outlined in Figure 6.5.

FIGURE 6.5   Digital Curriculum Evaluation Rubric

APPLICATION NAME: EVALUATOR NAME: SUBJECT(S): GRADE LEVEL(S): TYPE OF APPLICATION (EX: WEBSITE, IPAD APP)				
CATEGORY	NO	PARTIALLY	YES	HIGHLY
Is the curriculum aligned to the school's standards?				
Is the application aligned to the school's pedagogy?				
Is the program adaptive?				
Does the app assist in differentiating instruction?				
Is the application engaging and motivating to students?				
Is the app interactive and collaborative?				
Does the program build 21st-century skills?				
Is the program reliable?				
Is the user interface attractive and intuitive to use?				
Does the application provide valuable learning data?				
Is the data easy for teachers to understand and use?				
Does the application appeal to many learning styles?				
Is the program compatible with the school's devices?				
Is it easy to add, manage, and delete users?				
Does the program work with other programs used?				
Is the application free or affordable?				

LINKS TO LEADERSHIP: HELPING TEACHERS SELECT THE BEST-FIT DIGITAL CURRICULUM

For a successful transition to a digital curriculum, teachers need support in order to not become overwhelmed by the task of finding, evaluating, and curating digital content. Teacher trailblazers and leaders in leadership positions can provide this support through the following structures.

Build Capacity Through Committees

While teachers and departments can try out free resources in an ongoing manner without any costs to the school, paid providers should be reviewed for quality before purchase. Many of these providers allow for teachers and students to experience a portion of the services for free before upgrading.

Engage Students as Owners via Student Input

The concept of a teacher committee for curriculum selection is not new, but with the inclusion of students as content reviewers, the task of evaluating and selecting digital curriculum for a personalized learning environment can take a different form. As teachers experiment with different curriculum providers, they can leverage student input through a simple rating system. A survey tool such as Surveymonkey or Google Forms can help teacher trailblazers make recommendations to a curriculum committee for more formal review based on student engagement and perspective. Further, curriculum committees can use a similar tool to assess the teacher experience before making a more formal selection.

Build Capacity Through Professional Development

School leaders planning for professional development experiences can create time for teams to curate and create resources together. Teachers will benefit from sessions focused on how to

- assess the quality of digital curriculum;
- find digital curriculum aligned to instructional standards;
- make their own videos and screencasts; and
- share resources within their team via a collaborative document or other shared space like a Pinterest board.

DIGITAL CURRICULUM AND THE PLANNING PROCESS

Understanding the roles of teacher, student, and digital curriculum in a personalized learning model is an important starting point. An example of a

FIGURE 6.6 Co-Planning Roles for Personalized Learning

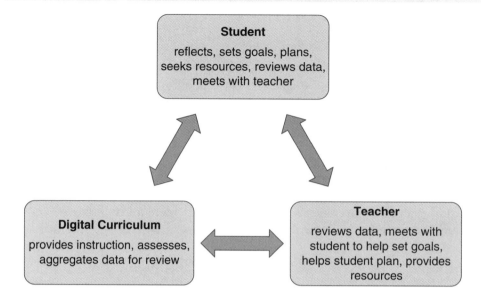

co-planning partnership between a teacher and student in a personalized setting is outlined in Figure 6.6. This illustration shows the role of teacher, student, and digital curriculum within a planning process so as to engage the student as a driver and owner of his or her learning. The flow of information between the three entities is multidirectional. In the driver's seat, the student learns from the teacher how to review learning data and reflect on areas of interest to set new goals, how to design strategies and learning experiences to achieve those goals, how to identify the best fit resources to use through the learning process, how to set a timeline and series of check-ins with his teacher, and how to engage in an iterative process of reflection, learning, and revision of the learning plan. In a coaching role, the teacher receives and reviews data from both the student and any digital curriculum platforms in use, guides the student in the design of the learning path, provides resources for the student to use, and frequently checks in with the student, providing additional instruction and guidance during the learning process. In this model, the teacher and student both interact with the digital curriculum, with the teacher reviewing learning data and suggesting pathways to the student for the next learning experience, and the student engaging in learning activities, reviewing performance data, and identifying upcoming learning experiences based on co-planning with the teacher.

ORGANIZING AND SHARING DIGITAL CURRICULUM

When integrating digital curriculum into classrooms, it is important to consider how to organize and share resources for easy, ongoing student access. Teachers organize resources in a face-to-face setting in numerous ways. Some curricular resources are shelved on labeled bookcases in class libraries, and are provided to students in the form of textbooks or hand-outs, or listed in a course outline. With a variety of digital resources at their disposal, teachers will benefit from forming an organization and sharing strategy for digital curriculum. By establishing a clear plan for sharing class resources, teachers alleviate the stress students may feel in trying to remember which website to go to in order to complete their work or learn. This organization saves teachers frustration from having to help multiple learners find their resources at the same time. The following are ways that teachers can consider sharing digital curriculum resources to establish a routine access path to them.

- Create and share a class resource folder within the LMS or using a tool like Google Drive. It is important to allow for viewing only within this designated folder so that students do not accidentally move resources out of the folder.

- Start a Pinterest board or Padlet on which to store links to frequently used sites.

- Create and share a personalized planning document with each student where both teacher and student can post a targeted skill and accompanying digital resource.

- Use Quick Response (QR) codes or shortened URL links to post frequently used resources on posters around the room and to course outlines. Tools like Google or Bit.ly can create shortened and customized URL links for easy listing.

- Help students create a favorites folder in their browser or desktop shortcuts to resource links.

- Use a tool like Drive or Evernote to help students create and maintain online binders for important class resources and their work.

LINKS TO LEADERSHIP: HELPING TEAMS PLAN TOGETHER

As teams transition to a blended learning environment, they benefit from time spent together in planning. During this time, they can review resources and determine the curriculum that's the best fit for their department or grade level. While it is not always feasible to create the amount of shared planning time needed for this task, it is possible to extend it through a shared planning document. Using a tool like Google Drive and Documents, teams can collaborate in the creation of a resource hub, linking instructional content they have either found or created for their classrooms. Teacher trailblazers are instrumental in exploring digital curriculum and sharing quality resources with the team in either shared planning sessions or documents.

DIGITAL CURRICULUM IN
BLENDED LEARNING MODELS

In the Whole Group Rotation, Station Rotation, and Flipped Classroom Models that we cover in Part 3, students engage with digital curriculum when they are not receiving direct instruction or collaborating with their peers on projects. When students are learning via digital curriculum, this often means that they are involved in independent learning at their own pace. In each model, the flow of students into and out of the use of digital curriculum varies as follows:

Whole-Group Rotation Digital Curriculum Integration

- The whole class moves into and out of digital curriculum or an online learning space at the same time within a class period. This means that teachers must have a plan for getting all students into the right space at the same time.

- This process can be for part or all of the period.

- While students are learning via digital curriculum, the main role of the teacher is to circulate around the room and coach students based on observation. This can also be a time when teachers individually workshop briefly with students on other learning tasks, or conference with them on their learning plans.

- The use of headphones for multimedia is essential for concentration of all learners.

Vignette: Kristen St. Louis, 7th Grade Student

Students at my school take a lab style class known as WRM (pronounced "worm"): writing, reading, and math Lab. During these specific class periods, we use our computers as a whole group during the entire period to work through personalized lessons. In math WRM lab, we use either Khan Academy or RedBird programs. Khan Academy has a variety of math topics to choose from, while RedBird has a specific plan that each student according to their grade level must do to advance. In the English portion of WRM Lab, we usually use IXL or WordVoyage programs—IXL focuses on a variety of topics the user chooses, and WordVoyage focuses on developing new vocabulary. As students, we have our own WRM Lab document on Google Drive that provides us with individual assignments for that class. It is possible for me to work on a completely different topic in IXL from the person next to me.

I appreciate this system because it allows for each person in the class to work on the specific skills they struggle with in order to understand them better. In addition,

I can go at my own pace in accomplishing the assignments and still be given the opportunity to understand the topic in its entirety. I can watch videos, learn from a step-by-step process shown on the digital program, or read a simple explanation of why I answered a question incorrectly. If I still do not understand the topic, then the teacher will halt their walking around to assist me. WRM Lab gives me the choice to decide which teaching style I would rather learn from, or how to learn from both the technology and my teacher.

Station Rotation Digital Curriculum Integration

- Students move into and out of digital curriculum in small groups within the rotation.

- Digital curriculum comprises a portion of the class period and one to two stations. This is balanced by other stations focused on other modalities of learning.

- While students are learning via digital curriculum, the teacher is stationed at the direct instruction or conference station. Other students are at the hands-on or project-based learning station.

- The use of headphones at the digital curriculum station is essential for multimedia.

Flipped Class Digital Curriculum Integration

- Students learn from digital curriculum at home prior to entering class.

- The role of the teacher is to provide the assigned digital content for home learning and a means of assessing student progress and achievement of the learning.

- In class, students may engage in digital curriculum via a class or lab rotation as a follow-up to the lessons obtained at home, but this is balanced by more time interacting with the teacher, engaged in hands-on learning or class discussions, and collaborating with peers.

The best place to begin implementing digital curriculum is where a problem exists for which the solution is provided by the integration of digital curriculum. This is especially important early on in the implementation of a blended learning model. Kim Weber, a 4th grade teacher at The Mandell School, shared how she and colleagues looked to implement digital curriculum to help differentiate word study.

While change can be difficult, the addition of digital curriculum has enhanced my instruction and my ability to meet the needs of all my students. Specifically, there was a need for a stronger and more differentiated vocabulary and grammar component in our curriculum. Since there never seems to be enough instructional minutes to accomplish personalized planning, we knew that digital curriculum could help us to achieve our goals.

We began researching online programs, knowing that we didn't want to hastily grab something that was simply the equivalent to online worksheets. We wanted the digital curriculum to provide content, personalization, and practice. We wanted the teacher to have control over vocabulary word choice and the grammatical instruction. We also wanted an assessment component.

We chose Word Voyage because it is a comprehensive vocabulary program that allows teachers to choose word lists from children's literature they are using in their classrooms. It provides teachers control over activities, such as roots, prefixes/ suffixes, parts of speech, just to name a few. Once students explore the linguistic components of the vocabulary word, they then write original sentences with virtual formative feedback from the teacher. Students work at their own pace and can be assigned to separate groups to target specific skills.

Once students started using the program, I saw the true value of this digital curriculum. Students were working at their level and receiving timely teacher feedback, which accomplished the goal of increasing vocabulary and improving grammar in a meaningful, integrated context. The use of technology in itself was a hook, but the features that allowed students to see their progress and accuracy provided them with more ownership and control over their learning. Students love the gauge on the side of the screen that indicates if they are completing work on pace for the end of the unit test. This feature develops their time management skills and fosters independence. In the end, this digital curriculum not only achieved the academic goals for our program, it saved planning time and allowed students to take an active role in their learning.

The best advice I can give teachers who haven't started to use digital curriculum is to begin with one program, a good one, that fixes or enhances a part of the curriculum that is lacking. Once I took this first step, I was able to identify other areas that lend themselves to digital curriculum and then find the resource to fit that need.

WRAPPING IT UP

Digital curriculum is distinct from apps and tools discussed in Chapter 5 in that the programs contain prepopulated learning content. Through digital curriculum, students receive instruction via multimedia videos or auditory components coupled with skills practice in adaptive platforms. Teachers can use digital curriculum to replace four types of offline learning tools: core textbook, supplemental textbook, lecture, or workbook. Digital curriculum helps to provide different pathways for individual learners in a personalized environment. Teachers can also build student agency through the use of digital curriculum by engaging students in the planning and data analysis process. Students can play a key role as stakeholders during pre-pilot and pilot stages, sharing feedback with teachers and digital curriculum committees to help assess the value of the program at scale. Similarly, teacher trailblazers play an important role in trying out new digital curriculum during the pre-pilot tinkering stage, and by making recommendations for larger scale implementation.

BOOK STUDY QUESTIONS

1. How do the types of digital curriculum outlined in the chapter compare with curriculum resources in use at your school? In what subject areas is it most feasible to make smooth transitions to digital curriculum via a pilot program?

2. What are the biggest benefits and/or challenges to using digital curriculum? Are there any challenges or obstacles you are concerned with that were not addressed in this chapter? If so, what were they and how can you overcome these challenges?

3. For your content area and grade level, what are the opportunities to use digital curriculum? What types of curriculum fit into your existing practice? What resources can you use to solve challenges you face as you transition to new blended learning models?

4. In what ways can teachers at your school be empowered to select and use digital curriculum, and make recommendations regarding digital curriculum?

5. What are the tradeoffs to using digital curriculum in place of more traditional instruction? For example, what does a teacher and student gain or give up watching a video instead of a lecture? How can you plan for these tradeoffs in a way that is comfortable for your class and your program?

6. What types of learning activities do you see as important to balance the learning experience in the use of digital curriculum?

CHAPTER 7

Assessment in a Blended Environment

I have a concrete example of what is expected, but also the creative freedom to showcase my skills and pursue my specific passions.

—Eva Oliveri, 11th Grade

WHAT DO WE REALLY MEAN BY ASSESSMENT?

Assessment is any means through which teachers can achieve a greater understanding of where their students are along their learning paths. The multiple forms of assessment are categorized as either formative or summative. Where the former is typically progress-oriented and a low-stakes measurement, the latter is more evaluative and a high-stakes dimension. For example, graphic organizers, exit tickets, skill practice, and project benchmarks are more formative in nature compared to unit tests, papers, or final project outcomes. In a blended learning environment, both formative and summative assessments remain relevant; however, the digital learning tools available make the daunting task of administering frequent formative assessments and collecting data more manageable to teachers. Many of these tools also enable diagnostic assessment to determine the best starting point for learning. Further, these tools create multidimensional and creative lenses for teachers to see evidence of learning and provide feedback on an ongoing basis, even down to the minute!

This chapter

- explores what motivates and drives student learning;
- outlines different forms of assessment data and provides strategies for using data;
- taps into assessment resources from Learning Management Systems (LMS) platforms;
- explores tools for assessing higher order and creative learning in a blended environment;

- outlines different forms of formative assessment;

- provides strategies for planning with formative assessment with feedback in mind; and

- examines some challenges of assessment in a blended learning environment and provides solutions for overcoming them.

The overall data management and assessment process should become progressively more frequent and personalized as schools move along the *Blended Learning Roadmap*. By Phase 3: Expansion, schools are reviewing data and making daily instructional adjustments at the student level.

WHAT DRIVES STUDENT LEARNING?

Before delving into the nitty-gritty of assessment, it's beneficial for school leaders and teachers to discuss what motivates and demotivates students to learn in their school. Taking time to examine the existing culture of motivation in a school, what is working to inspire students and what is in the way helps to form goals for high engagement and motivation at the school level. Digital platforms offer a variety of tools that teachers can use within this loop, some of which align with incentive and reward programs while others are designed to capitalize on creativity and communication motivation. Whether a school is more or less incentive driven, a certain number of both extrinsic and intrinsic motivators are in play. Therefore, the more important question becomes where to use one motivator versus another, and what balance is healthy for the desired culture within the school.

Research suggests extrinsic motivators work best for simple tasks which can be accomplished expediently without much creative thought. However, the opposite is true for creative, complex tasks. In a popular Ted Talk, *The Puzzle of Motivation*, author Daniel Pink makes the case against extrinsic motivators for complex, creative tasks. He cites research that suggests in situations which require complex, divergent thinking, rewards are ineffective and counter-productive motivators, while more intrinsic motivators, such as autonomy, mastery, and purpose are much more effective.

 If students are engaged as agents of their own learning, helping to set goals and choose learning experiences alongside their teachers, they can achieve an age-appropriate level of autonomy. Teachers can generate intrinsic motivation by providing students with a work model aligned with their individual learning preferences and talents. As educators have long recognized, students are much more motivated to engage in higher order thinking and working when learning is relevant and purposeful. Projects and experiences that put real-world problems at the forefront and tap into student passion or mastery provide an intrinsic catalyst for the best outcomes.

Educators also recognize other key motivators in place for students that operate on an innate level. The power of social motivation and an authentic audience cannot be overlooked. A quick peek into the world of fan fiction (fiction about characters or settings from an original work of fiction, created by fans of that work rather than by its creator) confirms this observation. Many writers feel not only inspired by their interest in this "fandom" subculture, but they also feel accountable to the writing community. Millions of teenagers are writing at a feverish, impassioned pace (sometimes at the expense of their assigned writing homework). When faced with this evidence of intrinsic motivation, it begs the question: *Why don't we see more of this in the classroom?* In a blended environment, opportunity exists to capitalize on this extracurricular trend, and move the needle on student learning. The same is true for other hobbies, such as gaming and hacking.

Many students trade in emotional currency; they yearn for validation and connection with a teacher who inspires them and believes in them. When technology can be used to bring teachers and students closer together in their rapport, motivation to learn is augmented. In planning for assessment within a blended learning environment, teachers can use their close knowledge of their students to align intrinsically motivating experiences which play off student talents and their sense of purpose. The incorporation of digital learning platforms that provide precise data on student learning complements this knowledge to allow a more comprehensive view of the student.

READING AND RESPONDING TO THE DATA NARRATIVE

In *UnCommon Learning,* Eric Sheninger discusses the way in which digital learning has enabled the unprecedented capacity for transparent assessment and student engagement. However, he also cautions that high student engagement does not necessarily indicate student learning.

> I have observed numerous lessons where students were obviously engaged through the integration of technology, but there was no clear indication that students were learning. Having fun, collaborating, communicating, and being creative are all very important elements that should be embedded elements of pedagogically sound lessons, but we must not lose sight of the importance of the connection to, and evidence of learning. (Sheninger, 2016, p. 66)

The hard work in personalizing instruction is to thus correlate learning outcomes, instruction, and digital tools on a dynamic continuum in order to enable students to move at their own pace. One way to overcome this challenge and ensure evidence of learning is to leverage student data from adaptive learning software and use it to inform instruction.

Adaptive learning platforms have gained popularity in blended learning classrooms as teachers have come to recognize the value of the data narrative to inform instruction and personalize learning. Not only do such platforms foster student agency by allowing some amount of control over pace and content, they also increase student motivation by enabling awareness of progress toward mastery through an instant feedback loop. Where time in between assessment and feedback used to rely on the ability of the teacher to review rapidly and provide such feedback, students and teachers are now able to track achievement benchmarks instantaneously. Both field experience and research indicate that this decrease in the feedback response time is important to higher achievement. The 2011 study "Timing Matters" by Opitz, Ferdinand, and Mecklinger analyzed the feedback timing factor between two groups, finding performance gain was significantly larger for the group receiving immediate feedback as compared to the group receiving delayed feedback.

Tiffany: The Power of Instant Feedback

@TeachOnTheEdge

When the Redbird Math adaptive software we use launched a new teacher dashboard, I stopped into the math classes to see it in action. In 30 seconds, I was able to witness the power of the data-informed feedback loop to motivate and personalize learning. We had just met with a parent of a student who was struggling in math that morning, and his teacher Lyman Casey shared that the student's biggest obstacle was confidence, that he needed to believe he could do it. When I walked into this student's math class, Lyman was monitoring the "Happening Now" feed which shows minute-by-minute progress. It showed that this student had gotten ten in a row correct and prompted Lyman to "go give him a high five!" Lyman quickly circled over to the student to do exactly that and offer encouragement to keep the good learning going. The student smiled a large smile in return and returned to focus on his problem solving.

LINKS TO LEADERSHIP: TOOLS AND TIME FOR MANAGING DATA

Leaders can help support teachers in interpreting the data narrative by providing time for this task and for teams to share information about students. Tools are hitting the market which enable aggregation and sharing of data through a one-stop data dashboard, such as Ed Elements's *Highlight*, which is a Personalized Learning Platform which has a number of integration partners to support this type of synthesis. However, these tools are dependent on the integration capacity, so before purchasing leaders should examine the fit of the tool with the digital curriculum in use. As data dashboard tools are just now becoming an industry priority, leaders may need to get creative in the meantime, building a school tool for simple data input into one place to provide the ongoing picture of each learner. Data teams can work together to determine which tools provide the richest assessment data, how to pull it and combine it, and how often to report it.

Maximizing the LMS

As discussed in Chapter 5, an LMS, such as Schoology or Google Classroom, can serve as an assessment hub, containing a variety of formative assessment tools and providing student access to performance data on a regular basis. The following are features of an LMS which empower the assessment and feedback loop:

- Polls—Teachers can check for understanding, gauge student interest, or form groups based on poll responses.

- Discussions—Through discussion tools, the whole class or individual groups can share ideas to extend learning. Teachers have the option to enable the grading tool for the discussion or to simply encourage participation.

- Rubrics—While there are great online tools teachers can use to create rubrics like *Rubistar,* it is now possible to do so within the LMS. The rubrics are simple to create and translate to the grade in the gradebook within the LMS directly so students can see their feedback and teacher comments.

- Mastery, Individual, & Small-Group Assignment—Within the LMS, it is possible align assignments to standards for mastery grading and to assign activities to individuals or small groups.

- Comments—When students submit work via the LMS (e.g., the Dropbox feature in *Schoology*), teachers can comment and annotate the documents, providing feedback for students.

- Gradebook—LMS platforms have a gradebook feature which can be set up according to the school's specific grading scale and preferences. It is possible to have this open to parents for viewing constantly, periodically, or never.

- Badges—Badges have become increasingly popular for recognizing achievement, especially in blogging spaces. Students may appreciate the extrinsic reward of a badge, especially if they help to design it and decide which indicators will be used to award it.

- Tests/Quizzes—The LMS provides tools for building tests and quizzes within the platform. It is even possible to enable autograding for objective questions and to manage when and how students can see their results, and/or retake an assessment.

FIGURE 7.1 Getting the Most Assessment Value From Your LMS

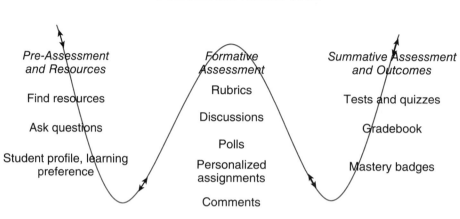

**Getting the Most Out of
LMS Student and Teacher Tools**

*Pre-Assessment
and Resources*

Find resources

Ask questions

Student profile, learning
preference

*Formative
Assessment*

Rubrics

Discussions

Polls

Personalized
assignments

Comments

*Summative Assessment
and Outcomes*

Tests and quizzes

Gradebook

Mastery badges

Beyond Grades and Data

Project-based and discovery learning play a significant role in a blended learning classroom. These types of assessment allow for a flexible time-line and the type of "rough synchronization" mentioned in Chapter 12 as effectively proven for high levels of online collaboration. Students can have a project to work on over the course of a specified period, and during this time work at their own pace during allocated project time, whether during a rotation experience at a project-based learning (PBL) station, or within an individual playlist schedule. Projects and discovery-based explorations, such as webquests or virtual field trips also serve as complementary assessments to the more data-driven adaptive platforms, and help teachers see the learner in a multidimensional manner. There are several digital tools teachers are using to amp up creativity in their classroom through project-based learning. For example, the "Padagogy Wheel" developed by Allan Carrington illustrates a number of such tools organized by Bloom's taxonomy and the SAMR (Substitution, Augmentation, Modification, Redefinition) technology integration framework. A live version of this tool is maintained at www.padagogy.net and can help teachers identify the tool aligned with their targeted assessment outcome.

Rubrics are essential tools in a project-based or discussion environment. Whether creating an infographic on *Piktochart,* contributing to a *Padlet* idea board, or writing on a class blog, students need to understand the standards used to measure their work and the expectations of performance around each standard. The creation of so many different rubrics can be a challenge for teachers. Figures 7.2 and 7.3 are examples of rubrics designed to be broad enough to apply to a number of learning experiences, categorized by type.

FIGURE 7.2 Communication and Sharing Rubric

	ONLINE BLOGGING/DISCUSSION RUBRIC (FOR USE IN LMS, BLOG, TWITTER BACKCHANNELS, TODAY'S MEET, PADLET, ETC.)			
	(4) EXCEEDS EXPECTATIONS	**(3) MEETS EXPECTATIONS**	**(2) PARTIALLY MEETS EXPECTATIONS**	**(1) DOES NOT MEET EXPECTATIONS**
What I Say	• is original and shows understanding • is supported by textual evidence • extends ideas • is ___ in length • contains extras like media, links, hashtags	• is thoughtful and shows understanding • is supported by evidence • extends ideas • is ___ in length	• is thoughtful and shows partial understanding • would benefit from more evidence • partially meets length and/or citation requirement	• lacks thought, understanding, or effort • is not supported • repeats rather than extends ideas • does not meet length requirement
How I Say It	• is elevated in academic tone and respectful • gives credit where due • is grammatically correct	• is appropriate for academic setting and respectful • gives credit where due • contains up to ___ errors	• is appropriate, but too casual in tone • may not give credit • contains up to ___ errors	• is too casual, inappropriate, or disrespectful • may not give credit • is not indicative of editing effort
How I Engage	• responds to ___ + users • engages in dialogue with peers • extends the thoughts of others through good questions and suggestions	• responds to ___ users • somewhat engages, but may not follow up with comments • mainly agrees or disagrees, but extends little	• responds to ___ users • could have more responses and engage in peer dialogue • would benefit from extending the ideas of others further	• does not meet required response minimum • does not interact with others and extend thoughts

FIGURE 7.3 Creative Project Rubric

	ONLINE CREATIVITY TOOL RUBRIC (FOR USE IN SLIDE PRESENTATIONS, MEDIA, INFOGRAPHIC, ETC.)			
	(4) EXCEEDS EXPECTATIONS	(3) MEETS EXPECTATIONS	(2) PARTIALLY MEETS EXPECTATIONS	(1) DOES NOT MEET EXPECTATIONS
Meat *What ideas are conveyed?*	• is original and shows understanding • is supported by textual evidence • cites ___ sources • is ___ in length • contains extras like media, links, hashtags	• is thoughtful and shows understanding • is supported by evidence • cites ___ sources • is ___ in length	• is thoughtful and shows partial understanding • would benefit from more evidence • partially meets length and/or citation requirement	• lacks thought, understanding, or effort • is not supported and/or does not properly cite • does not meet length requirement
Magic *Is it creatively presented?*	• shows highly creative, "outside the box" thinking • has that "wow" factor	• shows creative effort • is neat and impressively designed	• shows some creative effort • would benefit from more effort and attention to design	• does not show creativity, originality, and/or presentation effort
Mechanics *Is it well-edited and academic in tone?*	• is elevated in academic tone • gives credit where due • is grammatically correct	• is appropriate for academic setting • gives credit where due • contains up to ___ errors	• is appropriate, but too casual in tone • may not give credit • contains up to ___ errors	• is too casual, inappropriate • may not give credit • is not indicative of editing effort

Making It Personal

The closer teachers are able to get to a student's passion or optimum learning mode, the greater the opportunity to maximize gains. Providing students with experience using many tools is important to this process as students may not know of a tool unless required to explore it once or twice. However, where it is appropriate to then allow for student choice, the personalization of learning is enhanced. National Board Certified Teacher (NBCT) teacher and author Starr Sackstein encourages teachers to provide variety and choice in formative assessment practices. Starr's most recent book, *Hacking Assessment,* offers a number of creative assessment options for teachers to "go gradeless in a traditional grades school" (Sackstein, 2015, cover).

Teacher Vignette:
Starr Sackstein, NBCT @mssackstein

Find What Tool Works for Each Child and Let Them Use It

With technology changing rapidly over the last few years of my teaching career, I have found that different tools engage different learners. Rather than require any one tool for all of my students, I've realized the importance of using a variety to help engage them all.

As an English teacher, I have the luxury of unlimited formative opportunities to engage and assess student learning all of the time, and maximizing that potential is my business. For reticent students, we use Twitter as a backchannel for classroom conversation. Using the class hashtag #WJPSAPlit, students can contribute in meaningful ways in and out of class, asking questions, sharing resources, and engaging with each other.

In addition to Twitter chats and conversations, students write literature blogs in lieu of meaningless reading logs where they read books of their choosing and share reactions about writing, characters, themes, or make connections to their lives. They are taught and encouraged to comment using practiced feedback techniques on each other's blogs to enrich the classroom conversation about the literature we use in class. Blogger has been an easy addition, since the school is already using the Google Educational Suite for everything else.

Google docs has made the writing process more inclusive and meaningful. Students draft in this cloud-based platform and then feedback is provided through comments on their documents by me and other students and then revisions are made. Revisions can be tracked through revision history and students can literally see their drafts transformed when it comes time to reflect. In addition to a number of Google Chrome extensions for Google docs, we've also used Voxer, a free walkie-talkie app

(Continued)

(Continued)

to continue learning conversations as a dialogue. Students love to work with Voxer, to ask questions, and work through a dilemma with me rather than have to set up an appointment.

In addition to offering multiple ways of engaging students, assessments are always linked to deep reflection. Using Google forms, I'm able to gather data and then speak to students in class about their learning against the standards. For my students who prefer not to write everything out, they can do screencasts of their portfolios, walking me through their learning virtually, or send audio files that address specific learning. There is such a focus on depth of understanding that students are always meaningfully toiling with what they know and can do, and aren't focused on test grades or numbers. Instead, students regard progress through feedback that has been on-going, and specific to each of their needs.

The English classroom is no longer a silo for the solid few who like to read and can analyze, leaving the rest behind. Students show aptitude through movies, storyboards and comics, screencasts, papers, and tableaus. This year I even had a student make an entire movie in Minecraft and do voice-overs to explore their knowledge of A Christmas Carol. The English classroom isn't the only place for blended learning though. My journalism class on newspapers is completely blended as we create and run a student media outlet called WJPSnews.com. The students: organize using Google Sheets, write and provide feedback using Google docs, take pictures using their iPhones, record podcasts and interviews with their phones, and manage a site on Wordpress. A social media manager is responsible for our brand on Facebook, Twitter, and Instagram. All of these places ensure that the school is well represented and the students are learning real-world skills, which is often a result of their choices in the class.

LEADING AND LEARNING WITH FORMATIVE ASSESSMENT

When students enter a new grade level, they often carry one summative data point—their standardized testing data. Thus, this is sometimes the very first point from which learning is designed. However, when testing data precedes formative assessment, teachers understand the limitations of this data and the missed opportunity to understand the learner on a deeper level. Lower stakes and more frequent assessments of learning can illustrate more precise progress in skill development. Further, teachers are using formative assessment to gauge a variety of indicators beyond readiness and learning outcomes, including interest, grit, learning preference, and disposition toward learning. Table 7.1 outlines different types of formative assessments and some digital tools that enable them.

TABLE 7.1 Formative Assessment Types and Tools

BRAINSTORMING	WRITING	PRACTICING	SHARING
• polls • Bubbl graphic organizers • discussions • pictures, media	• blogs • shared documents • commemts, "suggesting mode"	• adaptive software • Socrative quizzes • Practice sites	• discussions • Padlet • social media posts • pictures, media

Planning with formative assessment in mind can be challenging, especially when students are working toward personalized goals. In an environment where there are many differences in the learning experience and path, it is helpful to establish routines and unifying anchors that help students navigate with clear expectations, and help teachers manage within these variables. Formative assessment templates help provide such an anchor. For example, the use of a Google form, which provides a template for students to record very different activities in the same format, can help teachers assess personalized progress in a similar fashion and see all entries in one place (see example at http://bit.ly/plearninglog1).

Choice boards, such as the Tic-Tac-Toe style illustrated in Figure 7.4, can be created with links to digital tools where applicable. These are helpful in ensuring balance of learning modes and environment, between online and face-to-face. Another template which can be created for broad use in the blended learning classroom is a rubric for rotation station work, discussion board participation, essays, or projects.

This choice board can be used for a number of different subjects with teachers specifying relevant content or changing out the tasks. Students can record their work by circling or highlighting the three options in a row that they select and then either linking their evidence of learning, or including it on the document.

FIGURE 7.4 Sample Choice Board

TIC-TAC-TOE YOU PICK 3 IN A ROW MAKE A COPY OF THIS SHARED DOCUMENT TO RECORD YOUR WORK		
Read (offline, learning)	Draw (offline, doing)	Present (offline, demonstrating)
Discuss (offline or online, demonstrating)	Write (offline or online, demonstrating)	Watch (online, learning)
Tinker (offline, doing)	Discover (offline or online learning)	Create (offline or online, doing)

How Can Formative Assessment Foster Student Ownership?

Formative assessment can empower ownership of learning when students are engaged in the process of planning for and reflecting on learning. Digital tools, such as an LMS or adaptive platform, offer more awareness of progress, allowing for more self-assessment and adjustment to meet goals. Other tools empower student agency through voice, with students contributing to and even leading discussions. The 2015 Harvard Business School study of online collaboration points to high effectiveness of peer to peer social learning, which substitutes for expert knowledge.

"When students struggled with a concept, we resisted (even more) the urge to jump in and correct the group, but relied on peers to do so. The results were remarkable (and somewhat humbling if you're an expert): in more than 90% of cases, questions were precisely and accurately answered by the peer group" (Anand, Hammond, & Narayanan, 2015, p. 1). Sharing planning documents between students and their teachers is another means to engage students as partners and drivers of their own learning. Some schools also cultivate student ownership by putting the student's voice at the center of conferences more traditionally experienced between parents and teachers in the absence of the student. For example, at The Mandell School in New York, students learn to lead their parent-teacher conferences so as to share their goals and strategies for actualizing them.

FIGURE 7.5 Common Assessment Challenges and Solutions

CHALLENGE	SOLUTION
Synthesizing multiple data sources	Select core tools to provide the majority of the data for analysis.
Tracking assignments	Use the LMS Dropbox or have students link their finished assignments to one shared document. The simple interface of the LMS and ability to grade and comment directly in the assignment field can greatly assist in tracking student work.
Sharing with parents	Communicate which tools will be used, obtain permission, and provide login credentials for those requiring online profiles for students under thirteen. Host a workshop for parents to receive training on digital tools. Having students teach their parents by showing them how they use the tools in class is a way to also strengthen both student agency and partnership. Provide a guide for parents to understand the digital tools and how to support their child (see Figure 7.6).

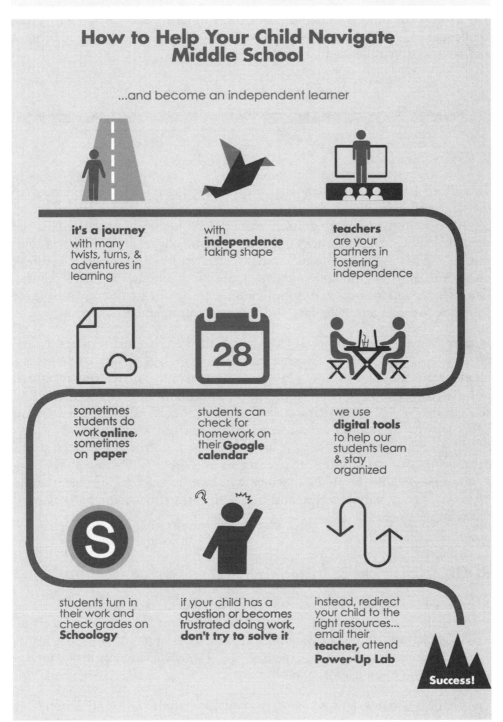

What Are the Challenges of Assessment in the Blended Environment?

The several advantages of digital assessment tools are accompanied by some challenges as well. Figure 7.5 (p. 90) outlines common assessment challenges and solutions in a blended learning environment.

WRAPPING IT UP

To get our best measure of how students are progressing, teachers need to see students' best efforts. Students are motivated to put forth their best by different incentives, ranging from extrinsic to intrinsic. Discussed in the opening chapter, the hallmarks of optimal blended learning are aligned with intrinsic motivators: autonomy (student agency); mastery (personalization); purpose (creativity, authentic audience); and peer interaction (connectivity). In a blended environment, this motivation can be augmented by immediate feedback through adaptive data and teacher reinforcement.

In addition to its motivational value, a blended environment offers a variety of tools for formative assessment. Students engage in formative assessments frequently and diversely, not only as a means of measuring progress, but also as learning itself. Whether participating in a discussion, creating something cool, or practicing a skill, students learn collaboratively with peers and teachers, and demonstrate their learning in multiple ways. As teachers and leaders consider the assessment tool kit they will use, it is important to keep core tools at the center so as to help teachers manage data and read the data narrative. Teachers can look to maximize tools like the LMS for its assessment value and build uniform rubrics for personalized pathways.

BOOK STUDY QUESTIONS

1. In what ways do you see students motivated or demotivated to learn and do their best in your school now? Think of ways that you can motivate students through agency, passion, purpose, social interaction, and rewards within your classes. Discuss the balance of intrinsic and extrinsic motivation within your school.

2. What assessment data is currently available within your school, and how are you using the data? What data would be useful to have? Explore adaptive tools which would provide this type of formative data.

3. If your school uses a Learning Management System, what tools are you currently using? Is there potential to maximize assessment and feedback value through increased use of the LMS tools?

4. How do you currently tap into higher order thinking in your classroom? Using a tool like the Padagogy wheel, discuss opportunities to digitize some of these assessments, or to explore new ones using digital tools.

5. Analyze the application of the rubrics for communication and project-based learning to a current assessment in your practice. Modify the rubric as needed to suit your classroom experience.

6. How are students involved in the assessment experience in your current practice? Discuss ways in which students can be further engaged as agents.

7. Which of the assessment challenges outlined in this chapter would be most relevant to your environment? Discuss solutions to these challenges.

CHAPTER 8

Onboarding and Supporting Students

I feel most creative when I am happy.

—Michael Saddler, 5th Grade

WHY DO WE NEED TO ONBOARD "DIGITAL NATIVES"?

The assumption that students, as digital natives, are instinctively "good at" technology can cause teachers to presume a higher level of competency and comfort using digital tools than students actually have. While it may be true that students have more familiarity in using tech tools, their skills may be more social and recreational. The skills required to succeed in an academic environment are related to those social skills; however, moving students into digital spaces under the assumption of readiness based on their recreational use of technology can set them up for failure. Further, as GettingSmart.com blogger Dave Guymon points out in "6 Mistakes You Might Be Making with Technology Integration," it is our responsibility to plan a bridge across the "digital divide" for students who do not have home access to the internet:

> Introducing a new device, app, or the internet itself still requires that we pay attention to equity issues and differentiation. . . . Incorporating support mechanisms for technology use into instructional designs and lesson plans is now just as important as doing the same for subject matter practice. Rather than viewing ourselves as 'Digital Immigrants' and our students as 'Digital Natives,' it would serve all of us well to accept the fact that we all are, in our own ways, 'Digital Explorers. (Guymon, 2014, para. 3)

In order for students and teachers to thrive in a blended learning environment, it is necessary to build capacity for both "Digital Explorer" groups through thoughtful onboarding practices. Students need skills specific to the different blended learning models we discuss in Part 3: Blended Learning—Exploring Classroom Models. For example, the face-to-face interactions of the rotation models provide more opportunity for hands-on teacher support as students build their digital learning competencies. For instance, if a student was struggling to submit work or complete assignments within a Learning Management System, a teacher would observe this struggle and intervene through a face-to-face conference. As students move into fully or mostly online classes like an *A La Carte Model,* their skillset must strengthen to accommodate the increased independence requisite to successful online learning. Schools can bridge this skill gap for students by first analyzing the skillset required in each environment, then creating a roadmap to build these skills through onboarding practices.

This chapter

- defines onboarding and how it applies to a blended learning setting;
- outlines the skills, training, and support students need for each blended learning model and how to define the expectations within each;
- applies Understanding by Design (UbD) framework to student onboarding practices;
  - Identify desired results
  - Determine assessment evidence
  - Design learning experience
- explores examples of student onboarding practices in action; and
- outlines strategies for embracing student mistakes as teachable moments.

Student onboarding is required through all three phases of the *Blended Learning Roadmap* as new tools are introduced, students transition from one grade to another, and new students enter the school. However, it is especially important to consider onboarding at the school level when moving from Phase 1: Foundations to Phase 2: Transitions.

WHAT DO WE MEAN BY ONBOARDING?

In the business world, the term "onboarding" refers to specific practices used by organizations to successfully help recent employees enter their new work environment. Through this process, employers strive to reduce any uncertainty and anxiety of the newcomers, help them make sense of their new environment, and provide them with the necessary tangible and intangible resources to become successful organizational members in their new role.

As schools introduce new digital platforms and tools, new learning environments are born, and in each case, students become newcomers to these environments. It is therefore beneficial to apply best practices in onboarding to these situations, strategically positioning students for success in their new workspaces.

School leaders and teachers can meet the three objectives of onboarding a group of students into a new environment through practices which provide training, opportunity to define behavioral expectations, and ongoing support. Figure 8.1 illustrates student outcomes and support structures that serve these three outcomes in a rotation or Individual Playlist Model, where the teacher has a substantial amount of face-to-face time with students and is able to monitor and respond to student needs within the classroom.

FIGURE 8.1 Onboarding for Primarily Face-to-Face Experiences

TRAIN	DEFINE	SUPPORT
• how to access digital tools and class resources • how to use new tools effectively • how to smoothly transition between activities • how to organize different digital spaces	• share objectives for using new tools • engage students in setting use expectations • connect digital citizenship learning to new tools • model and communicate community norms	• help students organize digital spaces • provide communication tools for students to reach teachers • monitor student interaction and engage in discussions • scaffold responsibilities to grow with students

This set of objectives and activities looks different in a model where students are primarily receiving instruction online. For a student to successfully complete an online course, the skills built in a primarily face-to-face setting are prerequisite while the following skills are even more critical:

- Ability to take initiative and work independently

- Time management and the ability to break down larger projects into their components

- Self-advocacy and resourcefulness in seeking help when needed

- Ability to troubleshoot minor tech issues (or access support) and use digital tools provided

- Ability to comprehend and apply learning material presented through video and written instruction

The expanded skill set for a primarily online experience mandates a different approach to onboarding and supporting students. Figure 8.2 outlines the student outcomes and support structures teachers may consider in orienting and training students for this type of setting.

FIGURE 8.2 Onboarding for Primarily Online Experiences

TRAIN	DEFINE	SUPPORT
• how to access course resources • how a login and participate in online discussions • how to seek help and communicate effectively • how to collaborate online	• course objectives and work expectations • teacher-student communication protocol • constituent (student, onsite facilitator, online teacher) responsibilities • class participation responsibilities and protocol	• help students organize deliverable deadlines • provide an onsite facilitator • monitor student interaction • promote peer leadership and expertise

Onboarding Through Effective Backward Design

We can apply McTighe and Wiggins' *Understanding by Design* (UbD) framework to designing the student onboarding experience: identify the transfer goals and essential questions, assess evidence of understanding and plan learning instruction for onboarding into each type of blended learning environment. In identifying the transfer goals for students in the introduction of new technology, teachers should view the gap as one in understanding and purpose rather than one of adoption. As digital natives, students are quick to adopt technology, but need to build a bridge which allows them to use it effectively in academic settings.

Tiffany: I experienced an adoption versus purpose gap myself a few years ago when first exploring Instagram with my students. I was new to Instagram and had a vision for the aesthetics of my feed, but a complete disregard for hashtags or likes. My students, on the other hand, were masters of sharing and cultivating a following. They liked my pics and schooled me on how to share effectively, link up with other like-minded "grammers," and build a community following. I was fascinated by their skillset, but couldn't help but notice their often complete disregard for content curation or purpose. Just as I couldn't answer their questions on why I didn't use hashtags, they couldn't explain what they were trying to say on their feeds.

We started a project together to explore the purposeful use of Instagram for social good, forming a feed for our "Finding Green" urban parks project and beginning a hashtag #findinggreennyc. Through this project, they taught me about sharing and community building, and I taught them about messaging and curating content by design. One of these students went on to establish a robust IG following of 60K+ users and is now an active member of a global photographer community with a highly marketable brand and skill.

Stage 1 of UbD Planning: Identify Desired Results

Using the training goals from Figure 8.1 as a starting point or launching pad for a mostly face-to-face environment, teachers can pose the following essential questions to students to begin to build this bridge:

- What similarities between the offline and online environments can we draw to further understand digital learning spaces?

- What opportunities are presented through the use of online learning, and what responsibilities accompany these opportunities?

- What is each person's role within a learning environment, and how do these look in both a face-to-face and online setting?

- What are the expectations for working with others offline, and how can we apply these to digital learning spaces?

- What skills from our experience as face-to-face learners can we apply to new online learning experiences?

- What can we do to maximize our learning in both face-to-face and online spaces?

- What can we do to stay connected with our teachers and get the support needed in both offline and online learning spaces?

Stage 2 of UbD Planning: Determine Assessment Evidence

Following the UbD model, teachers can move backwards from the target goals to determine evidence of understanding and a means of observing such evidence. For example, teachers should look for evidence, such as responsive communication, respectful dialogue, compromise, group focus, and shared responsibility for work product when positive productive online collaboration is the goal. The question then becomes: *How can teachers effectively assess this evidence?* There are numerous means of making this assessment, starting with observations and feedback from the same collaboration indicators in face-to-face interactions with the class. As students explore the essential question: *What are the expectations for working with others offline, and how can we apply these to digital learning spaces?*, teachers can have students form a group collaboration contract before working together, and then self-assess after collaborative learning in the face-to-face setting. From this practice, students can then draw connections to an online sharing space with teacher guidance. The use of a Venn Diagram or Look/Sound/Feel chart to explore the similar and different collaboration expectations between the two environments can also serve as an assessment of understanding.

Stage 3 of UbD Planning: Design Learning Experience

The learning experience can now be built from the evidence of understanding. Taking into consideration the aforementioned collaboration goal, it is advantageous to provide a learning experience that allows for both face-to-face collaboration and online collaboration so that students make the connection between effective practices in both spaces. Further, taking time between the two experiences to reflect on collaboration practices strengthens this connection as students move from one environment to the other.

For example, in science class, students may be tasked to work together on the design of a balloon-powered car, proceeding through the stages of collaboration and iteration in a face-to-face setting. The group can then move to a shared document or slideshow to collaborate on a summary and presentation. Prior to beginning, teachers should set the stage for how collaboration should look/sound/feel in the classroom and review guidelines for respectful communication and compromise in groups. Following the group work session, students can prepare for the transition to the online setting by making connections between the two forms of collaboration. Each facet of communication should be addressed, including purpose, tone, language, and inclusiveness. Figure 8.3 presents a flow of how this science lesson could transition through the two environments.

FIGURE 8.3 A Blended Workflow

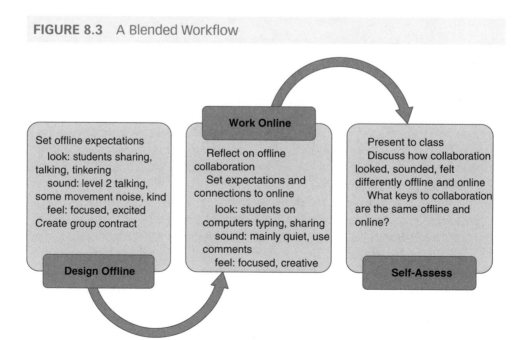

LINKS TO LEADERSHIP: ESTABLISHING A SCHOOLWIDE ONBOARDING PRACTICE

As technology instruction moves out of the silo of its computer lab origins, school leaders must establish schoolwide practices for instructing students on the academic use of technology tools by integrating the learning objectives into the school's curricular scope and sequence, and by allotting time for onboarding in the schedule each year.

We can safely assume the likelihood of a student taking an online course at some point in their academic careers. With the rise in K–12 online enrollment from just forty five thousand to over three million from 2000 to 2009, and a continued year over year increase expected since, this student experience may arrive well before college (Horn & Staker, 2011, p. 1). Keeping in mind the academic end goal of success in an online class, schools can design a crescendo of online learning beginning at an early age so that students build the skills needed to succeed in online learning over time and with teacher support in their face-to-face environments. In scaffolding this learning and building it into the program at a grade-by-grade level, school leaders need to consider how much time, in what subjects, and in what models the learning will take place. These considerations and probing questions are outlined in Figure 8.4.

FIGURE 8.4 Scaffolding Online Learning Curricular Integration

Proportion	How much time in each learning mode is ideal for the school's unique school mission and learning environment? For example, if a school's main modes of instruction are composed of teacher-based instruction, project-based learning (PBL), and computer-based instruction, a Kindergarten class may have a much smaller proportion of online learning than an Eighth-Grade class in the same school.
Subject	In what classes will each objective be met? For example, in scaffolding participation in online discussions, schools may focus initially on building this skill through book clubs in the literacy program, and then opening discussions in other subjects, later introducing peers outside the school, as students get older or more competent in their skills.
Schedule	Will learning take place solely in the classes, or will there be dedicated time to tech training? How will new students onboard into existing programs? For example, schools may integrate training into student orientation programs, or dedicate specific days of the year for this type of onboarding.

Build Capacity Through Student Trailblazers and Buddy Programs

In the same way that teacher trailblazers are vital to building capacity in faculty culture, so too are student trailblazers vital in sampling the proper use of technology in class. Students who are quickly able to understand and use platforms can provide guidance and modeling for their peers or younger students. Buddy programs which pair an older and younger class are a great way to build community and capacity for onboarding students into platforms for online learning. For example, older students could help coach younger ones using a math software like Khan Academy in a math buddy program.

 ## Engage Students in Peer Support Systems

As students build aptitude for using technology in an academic setting and an understanding of the unique blended learning culture of their school, they can emerge as partners in ongoing technology support. A student-run help desk is a great way to empower students in shared responsibility around technology integration.

Leader Vignette: Tiffany Wycoff, Academic Bootcamp

@TeachOnTheEdge

Since stepping into the role of school leader in a blended learning environment, I build in time for onboarding practices throughout the year. While much is integrated into the regular schedule, I achieved success by providing a few experiences dedicated to technology training and expectation definition. One of these constructs is what we call the "Academic Bootcamp" day at the beginning of each year.

Academic Bootcamp takes place the first week of school and is a dedicated day to building universal skills to help students succeed for the year. Some of the skills change year to year while others are consistent due to their core nature; however, all are applicable across disciplines.

	CONSISTENT	VARIES YEAR TO YEAR
Platform Use	Google Drive—Organizing Calendar Documents—Sharing and Collaborating Schoology—Discussions Schoology—Work and Grades	Prezi Instagram Google Sheets Google Forms Padlet iMovie Quizlet
Digital Citizenship	Explore and Define Collaborate on a Digital Citizenship or Class Contract	
Academic Skills	Study Skills (approaches vary from art integration to more traditional forms) Academic Integrity	Learning Style Inventory Sketch Notes Outlining Research Paraphrasing

To keep scheduling changes to a minimum for the day, each discipline is assigned one objective to cover. All the math teachers might cover Calendar, the English teachers Drive, history teachers Schoology discussions, and so on. The visual arts or performing arts teachers participate by incorporating study skills in the style of their art (i.e. sketchnoting, visualization, or use of song).

At our school, we use one day for this, but it would also work to spread it out over a week or a couple days, especially if a block schedule is in place. For elementary school children, introducing one application at a time over a longer period of time is more developmentally appropriate. This way, students can get used to one tool and build proficiency in using it before learning a new one.

Embracing Teachable Moments

In a blended learning environment, there must be a conscious effort to engage with students in digital spaces and to encourage them to explore within established age-appropriate boundaries. There is also a recognition that students sometimes step beyond these boundaries, using technology in ways that violate the school's honorable use agreement. Educators can model and practice exemplary interaction within learning spaces, drawing connection to social media use outside of school. In more traditional settings, students can only draw from their social media experiences, and chances are that there are few if any adults modeling the correct behavior for the child.

The goal of onboarding students is not to eliminate mistakes altogether. Inevitably, students make mistakes as they learn to navigate both learning and social spaces as digital citizens. School leaders and teachers should anticipate and embrace these moments as fail-forward opportunities. The digital exploration boundaries should expand as a child grows older much in the way that explore-alone boundaries in the community expand as a child ages. For example, a child living in New York City first learns to navigate his immediate neighborhood, perhaps traveling a few blocks home from school on his own by fifth grade. In the years between this milestone and high school, he likely learns to navigate most of the city via the complicated network of subways so that he can confidently and safely travel to and from a school, which is unlikely to be a neighborhood school. Children benefit from the same type of expanding exploratory nucleus in the digital world, with the idea that they navigate an area of relative safety through the age-appropriate circumference. By setting up social learning spaces like discussion boards where both teachers and students interact online, schools provide such a supervised circumference for students to learn how to interact with others online. When mistakes are made within this space, an adult is there to help the child reflect on the error and learn forward from the failure.

Parents can become fearful of potential risks as schools incorporate social learning spaces into their curriculum. It is important for school leaders and teachers to build an understanding and appreciation for the digital world's teachable moments into the teacher and parental culture of the school. Here are some ways to accomplish this:

- Incorporate commitment to growth mindset in the Honorable Use Policy (as opposed to zero-tolerance).

- Ensure teachers are able to monitor and engage in school digital community spaces so that when students post something of concern, there is awareness of the interaction and an opportunity for teachers to redirect and model a better standard for interaction.

- In parent workshops, help parents understand the benefit of the "growing nucleus of exploration," and engage them as partners to help build this nucleus.

- Encourage parents to create honorable use policies with their children in a Digital Home Contract.

- Encourage parents to reference age regulations from social media sites to set boundaries for children. Parents often feel pressured to allow underage use of social media sites because "everyone is doing it." A family account can be a great compromise for usage and can open an opportunity for modeling, discussion, collaborative learning, and shared responsibility.

- When mistakes happen, take time to explore the situation through meaningful dialogue with the students involved so that reflection and learning can take place.

WRAPPING IT UP

As much as today's children use technology, there is still a need to instruct them on the purposeful use of it in an academic setting. The management of online resources and learning platforms can present new challenges for students and require support from teachers. As schools incorporate blended learning models into the curriculum, it is valuable to keep these support needs in mind and as they are introduced to create a protocol for onboarding students into new digital tools. Onboarding practices include training activities, outlining of expectations, and structuring ongoing support.

There are many benefits to such a practice, including increased student confidence and comfort in the space, more efficient implementation and faster launch to learning, clearer expectations between offline and online spaces, and further development of 21st-century skills. School leaders and teachers can use backward design in planning onboarding activities and assessments to meet the targeted outcomes. Schools should consider both the short-term and long-term goals and skills students need to succeed in online classes in the future as they design onboarding practices for students.

BOOK STUDY QUESTIONS

1. What are some of the assumptions teachers and school leaders make about students and technology? How can we challenge these assumptions?

2. What are some tech skills students seem to have before they enter your class? Are there students who have not developed these skills? How can you plan to differentiate onboarding?

3. What are the uses of technology where you see students sometimes falter or struggle? Think of one activity to help strengthen that skill for students.

4. What types of onboarding practices are ideal to start with in your school given the current state of blended learning? What practices are important to consider as your school's blended learning practices evolve?

5. What similarities can be drawn between helping students adjust to a new classroom and a new digital learning space? What current practices do you use to introduce students to your class which could be used to acclimate students to an online space?

PART 3

Blended Learning: Exploring Classroom Models

Catlin R. Tucker

INTRODUCTION

I entered the classroom in 2001 at the age of 22 excited to create the classroom I had been fantasizing about in credential school. In my elaborate fantasies, students bounded through my door eager and excited to learn. We were going to sit in a circle and talk about literature and life.

Needless to say, the reality was very different from my fantasies. Instead of bounding through my door, students trudged into my classroom. Instead of engaging in conversation, they sat silent, unwilling to take risks. I was crestfallen. I was failing. I could not figure out what I was doing wrong. I used all of the tools I was taught with, and all the tools I was taught to teach with, yet I couldn't get my students to take an active role in the classroom.

Seven years into my teaching career, I was at a breaking point. I remember thinking, "I have wandered into the wrong profession. Becoming a teacher was a monumental mistake." I decided to take a year off when my first child was born. During my year at home, I taught online college-level courses and was intrigued by several aspects of online learning. When I returned to the classroom, I decided to incorporate some of these online elements into my very traditional and very low-tech classroom.

I began with asynchronous discussions, because traditional discussions tended to fall flat. The same four or five students dominated real-time discussions in class and everyone else avoided eye contact, unwilling to participate. I must be honest; I was terrified of what 158 teenagers would say and do when let loose on the Internet, but I realized that nothing would change if I allowed fear to dictate my decisions.

So, I posted my first online discussion question. Within twenty minutes, the first three students responded—and all three were students who never talked in my class. I was stunned. These kids clearly wanted a voice in my class, but I had not given them a comfortable place to express or share their voice. This moment was a game changer.

I was excited by the power of technology to engage my students and help them to find their voices. I began experimenting with other strategies and technology tools. Despite working in a low-tech classroom, I embraced a BYOD (bring your own device) model and began designing Station Rotation lessons. I began using the Flipped Classroom Model to flip my vocabulary and writing instruction. I was blown away by how easy it was to place students at the center of learning when we used technology.

This section focuses on the individual blended learning models that teachers can use to weave together the best aspects of face-to-face and online learning to allow students more control over the time, pace, place, and path of their learning. The chapters in this section explain the models, suggest strategies for implementation, provide classroom examples, identify common challenges, and present creative solutions to meet those challenges.

Although this chapter is focused on supporting teachers in implementing the model[s] that will work best for them, there are links to leadership throughout.

CHAPTER 9

Station Rotation Model

What learning should look like is up to perception. Learning shouldn't be the same for every student, in every school, everywhere. Learning, at the end of the day, is knowing and benefiting from knowledge you are given; the ways in how you receive that knowledge are endless.

—Anaya Akpalu, 7th Grade

WHAT IS THE STATION ROTATION MODEL?

The Station Rotation Model is a subcategory of the Rotation Model, which is defined as "a course or subject in which students rotate on a fixed schedule or at the teacher's discretion between learning modalities, at least one of which is online learning" (Clayton Christensen Institute, 2015, p. 1). The Station Rotation Model does exactly what the name suggests—students rotate through learning stations in the classroom. At least one of the stations must be an online learning station for this to be considered a blended learning model. However, teachers with ample access to technology can design multiple learning stations using technology.

The Station Rotation Model offers a clear avenue for traditional schools and teachers to integrate online learning into the classroom setting, even if they have limited access to technology. Teachers can use this model to create small learning communities within the larger class setting, design differentiated tasks to challenge various skill levels, and spend more time working individually with students.

Instead of one-size-fits-all instruction where students move lockstep through a lesson, a teacher can use the Station Rotation Model to design dynamic learning station activities that employ different learning modalities and allow for more differentiation and individualization to improve comprehension, retention, and the students' ability to apply information.

This chapter

- highlights the benefits of the Station Rotation Model;
- presents creative solutions to meet the challenges of using the Station Rotation Model;
- provides strategies for designing Station Rotation lessons;
- shares example lessons to help teachers conceptualize a Station Rotation Lesson;
- identifies logistical concerns teachers should consider; and
- discusses grouping strategies.

Schools can look to implement the Station Rotation Model in either Phase 1 or Phase 2 of the *Blended Learning Roadmap,* depending on its similarity to the current teaching model. The Station Rotation Model may provide a more incremental Phase 1 option for many elementary classrooms already familiar with learning centers, while it may make sense in Phase 2 for middle and high school teachers who do not currently use learning centers.

WHAT ARE THE BENEFITS OF THE STATION ROTATION MODEL?

In a Station Rotation Model, students have more opportunities to take ownership of their learning. They ask questions, engage in discussion, and participate in a smaller group dynamic. This effectively places students at the center of learning because they are responsible for driving the learning at each station. In turn, the teacher has more opportunities to lead small group instruction, assess student understanding, and provide individualized support and feedback.

The three main benefits of using a Station Rotation Model instead of the traditional approach to teaching are that it

1. creates smaller learning communities within the larger class;
2. employs a variety of tasks and activities to increase engagement and allow students to engage with information in different ways; and
3. makes it possible for teachers to spend more time working directly with individual students to improve learning outcomes and individualize their teaching.

Figure 9.1 identifies specific benefits of using the Station Rotation within the context of these three larger advantages.

FIGURE 9.1 Specific Benefits of Using the Station Rotation Model

Create Smaller Learning Communities Within the Larger Class	• Students have more opportunities to ask questions and receive individual feedback as they work. • Small group activities are student-centered requiring that students actively participate to accomplish a task. • Activities can be differentiated to challenge various skill levels. • Students can control the pace of learning in a particular station. • Teachers don't need a class set of devices for this model to be successful. Because students rotate in smaller groups, only a few computers or student devices are needed at the online learning station[s].
Design Varied Tasks to Increase Engagement	• Kids love to move, so the very act of rotating around the room helps keep them engaged. • Adaptive technology adjusts activities based on individual student performance to provide personalized practice and review. • The variety of activities and learning tasks used in this model keeps student interest high. • Activities can incorporate different learning modalities to appeal to multiple intelligences.
Work Directly With Students and Individualize Teaching	• Teachers can review concepts, model processes, or provide direct instruction for small groups in the teacher-led station. • Teachers can get a better sense of what students know and understand so that they can tailor work to meet each student's learning goals. • Teachers have more time to work individually or in small groups with students to provide more individualized teaching as well as effective support and feedback.

Valerie Strauss wrote an article in *The Washington Post* about Howard Gardner, the John H. and Elisabeth A. Hobbs Professor of Cognition and Education at the Harvard Graduate School of Education and author of *Frames of Mind: The Theory of Multiple Intelligences*. In her review, she recommends that educators "learn as much as you can about each student and teach each person in ways that they find comfortable and learn effectively" and cites Gardner as pointing out that "this is easier to accomplish with smaller classes" (Strauss, 2013, para. 12). To find out what works best for each student and individualize their teaching, teachers without the luxury of small classes can use the Station Rotation Model to create smaller learning communities within the larger class. Add technology's ability to personalize learning, and students have a better chance of being successful academically.

In addition to encouraging teachers to individualize their teaching, Gardner encourages teachers to teach "important materials in several different ways, not just one"; he suggests teaching important material via stories, music, art, role play, diagrams, etc. to "reach students who learn in different ways" (Strauss, 2013, para. 13). Gardner calls this pluralizing teaching. Teachers using the Station Rotation Model can use a variety of strategies to cover material in the various learning stations to ensure that students have more than one way to engage with important concepts and information.

STATION ROTATION MODEL CAN TAKE MANY FORMS

The Station Rotation Model can take many forms depending on the teacher's approach. Figure 9.2 depicts an example of a Station Rotation lesson composed of four separate stations: teacher-led, collaborative student-centered work, individual practice with adaptive software, and makerspace.

In trainings, teachers often ask "Is this right? Am I doing this correctly?" It's important that educators feel free to adapt this model to best meet the needs of their specific student population. It must also work within the confines of their school structure and schedule, so it's vital to emphasize the flexibility of this model. There is no perfect number of stations or single way to implement the Station Rotation Model. Depending on the school schedule and the amount of time each teacher has with his or her class, students may move through a series of stations in one class or over several classes. The structure is pliable, allowing for many variations.

The main difference between traditional learning stations and the Station Rotation Model is that at least one station must be an online learning station.

FIGURE 9.2 Example of a Station Rotation

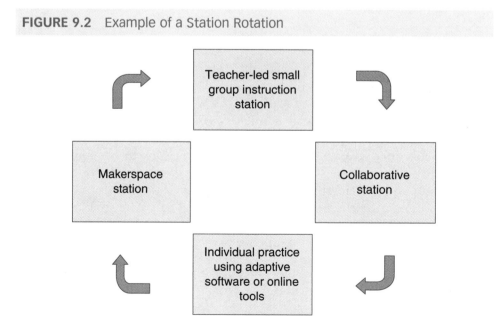

The online component can take many forms ranging from students using dynamic creation tools, to researching topics, to utilizing adaptive software. The focus of the online station depends on the objectives of the lesson. The addition of an online component requires that teachers have access to technology in some form or another to execute the Station Rotation Model in their classrooms. However, teachers in low-tech classrooms with only a few computers or devices can successfully use this model by creating one station with the devices available.

LINKS TO LEADERSHIP: ACCESS TO TECHNOLOGY

Leaders in leadership positions must anticipate and plan for the logistical challenges of shifting to the Station Rotation Model. For example, teachers need access to devices and the internet to ensure at least one of their learning stations is an online learning station. Here are some questions to consider when thinking about technology:

- Does the school have a budget for hardware? If so, how many devices will each teacher have access to in his or her room?

- What type of devices do the teachers want? How can you survey teachers to find out the technology best suited for their students and subject area?

- Do students need additional equipment, like headphones, to work online? Is there an ongoing budget for maintaining devices, equipment, and purchasing apps?

- Is there a budget for purchasing adaptive software to support personalized practice?

- Does your school allow students to bring their own devices or technology (BYOD or BYOT)? If so, can your school's infrastructure support the devices students are bringing to school if teachers want to encourage students to use their devices for learning?

- How can teachers and students easily access technology? What are the necessary check-in and check-out procedures? How can you facilitate equity of use?

Planning a Station Rotation Lesson

Learning stations are not a new concept in education, especially at the elementary level, so the Station Rotation Model is a natural extension for teachers who are already using learning stations. However, teachers who rely primarily on lecture or whole group instruction may find the shift from whole group to small group learning activities challenging to plan and implement. Not only does the teacher's approach to lesson design change, but the role of the teacher during the lesson also changes.

When planning a Station Rotation lesson, some teachers opt to begin as a whole class to outline the activities in each station, review expectations, articulate the goals for the day, and distribute any necessary materials to the whole group. However, teachers who are short on time and do not want to spend five to ten minutes frontloading the lesson can print out instructions for each station, create viewable Google Documents with links and resources, or record short video tutorials for students to watch at each station that explain what students need to do at that station.

Stations in this model can be composed of a variety of different activities. Here are some examples of the types of stations a teacher might use in the Small Group Rotation Model:

- Teacher-led small group instruction
- Collaborative small group work
- Makerspace
- Computer time with adaptive software
- Project-based learning time
- Online research
- Design and create (presentations, infographics, storybooks, etc.) with web tools
- Individual work or one-on-one tutoring with the teacher
- Virtual fieldtrips
- Role playing and/or performance
- Play review games on or offline
- Guided peer practice
- Small group discussions
- Review/practice activities

Figure 9.3 depicts a general Station Rotation Model. In this example, the groups rotate through each of the four learning stations: a teacher-led station, a collaborative group work station, a project-based group work station, and an online learning station. These stations do not build on one another, so the order of the rotation is not important.

FIGURE 9.3 Example of a Station Rotation

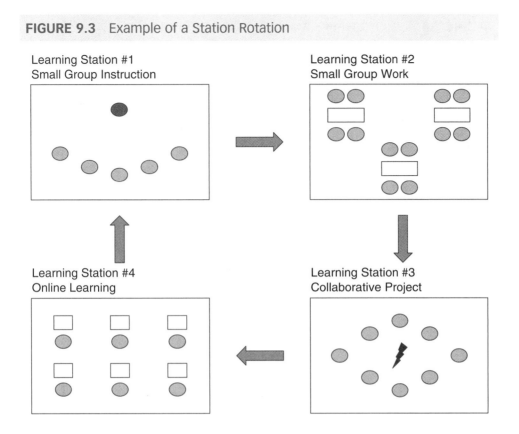

Learning Station #1
Small Group Instruction

Learning Station #2
Small Group Work

Learning Station #4
Online Learning

Learning Station #3
Collaborative Project

Although Figure 9.3 shows four stations, the number of stations can vary depending on the lesson. There isn't a perfect number of stations. Some teachers design three stations, while others prefer six. Teachers may decide on a specific number of stations because that's how many individual activities they have prepared, or they may make the decision based on how much time they have.

Station Rotation Lesson Template

Figure 9.4 pictures a basic lesson template teachers can use when designing stations. It's helpful to lay the various stations out visually because the order of the stations is important to consider when designing a lesson. Students don't visit the stations in the same order so the work at one station cannot build on the previous station. However, teachers can design Station Rotation lessons that span a series of days with one station building on the previous day's work.

Catlin: I often plan the number of stations based on the number of students I want in each station. For example, I typically plan four or five stations for a class of approximately twenty-eight students. If I have four stations, each group has seven students. If I plan five stations then each group has five or six students. Those numbers are manageable for high school-age students. Teachers working with younger students may want more stations to keep the number of students at each station lower to avoid distractions.

FIGURE 9.4 Class Rotation Lesson Template

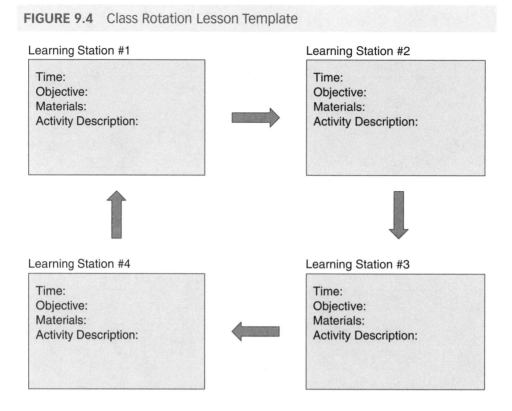

Learning Station #1

Time:
Objective:
Materials:
Activity Description:

Learning Station #2

Time:
Objective:
Materials:
Activity Description:

Learning Station #4

Time:
Objective:
Materials:
Activity Description:

Learning Station #3

Time:
Objective:
Materials:
Activity Description:

Teachers also want to consider their student population when deciding how groups progress through a series of stations. Some students may benefit from beginning with small group instruction before moving onto practice. While other students, who are accelerated learners or tactile, may learn better by starting with a practice activity where they get to explore and practice before they receive direct instruction. The teacher-led station for accelerated students may shift from instruction to a question-and-answer session with the teacher.

LINKS TO LEADERSHIP: HELPING TEACHERS TO MEET AND OVERCOME CHALLENGES

A teacher shifting from a traditional teaching model to the Station Rotation Model needs support from both teacher trailblazers and leaders. This model requires organized stations with clear learning objectives, classroom management strategies, and a plan for quickly and efficiently moving students around the room.

A teacher new to the Station Rotation Model benefits greatly from working with teacher trailblazers who are already comfortable planning and implementing this model in their classrooms. These teacher trailblazers can offer teachers who are just getting started with blended learning the opportunity to observe their classrooms to see what the Station Rotation Model looks like in action. Observing a lesson where students move to various learning stations helps teachers to conceptualize how lessons are designed and executed, as well as how the classroom is laid out to support this blended approach.

Building Capacity

Leaders can support teachers by arranging for professional development focused on supporting them in implementing the Station Rotation Model. Once teachers on the school site are using this model, it's beneficial to provide teachers time during the school schedule to observe the teacher trailblazers on their school site employing this blended learning model. This requires that leaders do the following:

- Arrange for substitutes and substitute pay to allow teachers to observe the teacher trailblazers on their campus.

- Organize a schedule for classroom visits and communicate clear expectations for these visits.
  - Will teachers meet ahead of time and/or debrief after the observation?
  - Will the teachers who are observing be asked to reflect on the experience?
  - Will the teacher trailblazers be asked to observe the teachers just getting started with blended learning to provide mentorship, coaching, co-teaching, and/or feedback?

Additional Staffing or Parent Volunteers

One last challenge that leaders should consider is whether or not there is funding for teacher aides or assistants to support the Station Rotation Model. This model requires that students move from one station to another. The teacher may choose to provide small group instruction at one station, which limits his or her ability to assist students working in other stations. A part-time teacher aide or assistant can help facilitate an additional learning station, or answer questions as they float around the room, or provide support. This is particularly helpful at the elementary level because younger students need more support and supervision.

Hiring additional personnel can be a significant expense that may not be realistic for your district, so school leaders may want to initiate a parent volunteer program or establish a volunteer requirement per family at the school (i.e., ten hours per child per year) to encourage parents and grandparents to donate time to the classroom as teaching assistants to achieve small learning communities.

Tip for Designing a Station Rotation:
Go Horizontal With Your Traditional Agenda

Teachers planning a Station Rotation can approach lesson design in a couple of different ways. For teachers just beginning to blend, we recommend "going horizontal" with your agenda to conceptualize how a Station Rotation can replace a traditional lesson. At first, it is easier to take a traditional whole group lesson and break it into parts that can be used to design the individual stations.

For example, in an early elementary class a traditional lesson might include these activities:

- welcome and sing songs;

- review a math problem as a class then students complete practice problems;

- read a story and answer questions about the characters and events in the story;

- draw a picture and write a few sentences describing the picture or tell a story about the picture; and

- complete an art project where students color, cut, and paste.

The transformation of this traditional agenda into a Station Rotation Model is illustrated in Figure 9.5.

FIGURE 9.5 Station Rotation Lesson

Math Station	**Teacher-Led Reading Station**
Watch a short video of the teacher reviewing a math problem, then practice math using an adaptive software program.	Listen to the teacher read a story then answer questions about the story. Note: Differentiate with more challenging books and questions for different groups.

Art Station	**Draw and Write Station**
Follow simple directions to color a picture, cut the parts of the picture out, then paste them carefully in a particular order on a colorful piece of construction paper.	Draw a picture then write a few sentences describing the picture or use the drawing to inspire a short story.

Many elementary teachers use stations on a regular basis, like the one pictured in Figure 9.5, so the challenge may not be in designing a lesson, but rather deciding how to leverage technology to transform one station into an online learning station. The key is to make sure that the addition of technology enhances and improves the activity because it allows students to pace their own learning, differentiates instruction, or personalizes practice. Teachers should never use technology for technology's sake. If it doesn't improve the activity or lesson, teachers should not add technology to a station.

It's often at the secondary level where teachers have a harder time transitioning from a traditional lesson to a Station Rotation Model. In part this may be due to the fact that more middle schools and high schools spend time delivering direct instruction. Often the teacher is lecturing and students are taking notes. Unfortunately, this approach to teaching relegates students to the role of passive receivers of information. The Station Rotation has the potential to shift students into active and engaged learners.

In my high school English class, which is a ninety-minute block period, a traditional agenda might look like this:

- Mini-lesson: How to write an argumentative paragraph
- Begin a draft of an argumentative paragraph
- Discuss Chapter 5 in *Of Mice and Men*
- Read and annotate an informational text related to migrant workers

To transform this traditional agenda into a Station Rotation, it looks like the image in Figure 9.6 (p. 121).

Vignette: Paloma Velasquez, 10th Grade Student at Windsor High School

All students, regardless of age, can relate to the traditional classroom routine of listening to a teacher lecture followed by some sort of whole class "engaging activity." For the students, this translates into a lot of time spent focusing on a single activity, which stretches our attention spans to the point of boredom. However, walking into Mrs. Tucker's class as a bright-eyed freshman, I realized this was not the only way to teach. Mrs. Tucker implemented something that I had never experienced before: the Station Rotation Model.

At first, I had to adjust to the expected speed to accomplish each activity, but it was nothing unreasonable as it merely required that we remain on task the whole time to complete the activity in a given station. Even my mind, which is constantly

(Continued)

(Continued)

teeming with activity, remained concentrated on each task because the station times are simply not long enough for me to get bored. The tasks were also very different. One station might be focused on an online activity, such as researching a topic and crowdsourcing information, completing a grammar review on NoRedInk, (an online tool for teaching grammar), or exploring collections in the Google Art Project. The other stations might require that we work together as a group, partici-pate in a discussion, or work directly with Mrs. Tucker. That variety is key.

Furthermore, there is an element of collaboration that results from this model since it is student-directed activity that depends on students in each group reading direc-tions and coming to a consensus as to what they have to do at that station. Each time we participate in a Station Rotation, there is an opportunity for a different stu-dent to take a leadership role in reading directions and guiding their group of peers.

I also feel this is an excellent way to design a class because it maximizes the little time we have together in the classroom. The transitions are more efficient than transitions in my other classes where the whole class moves to the same activity together and four lessons are taught in the span of a single hour. I have grown as a student as a result of participating in this model, not only in the knowledge gained in each station, but also in my time management skills and applied leadership techniques.

FIGURE 9.6 Redesigned English Lesson in Station Rotation Model

In-Class Flip Station	**Teacher-Led Writing Station**
Watch the "How to write an argumentative paragraph" video and take Cornell Notes.	Write the first argumentative body paragraph for your essay with teacher support and feedback.

Small Group Discussion Station	**Differentiated Reading Station**
As a group, crowdsource a list of questions you'd like to discuss about Section 6 in *Of Mice and Men*. Use those questions to guide your student-led discussion.	Read the Smithsonian Tween Tribune article and use *Diigo* to annotate the digital text. Please share annotations with me via email.

Design a Station Rotation to Target a Specific Skill

For teachers who are frustrated by large class sizes composed of various skill levels, this approach creates smaller communities within the larger class and allows for more opportunities for differentiation. Stations can be set up to challenge specific ability levels, which is why it can be helpful to consider designing a Station Rotation lesson that targets specific skill levels. The progression pictured in Figure 9.7 helps guide a teacher through the process of identifying a skill, selecting a grouping strategy, designing learning activities, and incorporating technology to personalize learning.

Begin by identifying the target skill and learning objectives for the Station Rotation lesson. Once you know what skill or skills you want to target, then you can decide on a grouping strategy that makes sense given your class population and the objective of the lesson. (For more on grouping strategies, see page 125.) Some activities may benefit from a mix of skill levels or learning modalities, while others may work better if groups are composed of students at similar skill levels or learning styles.

It's also important to think about how many stations students will visit in a day or class period. This depends on the target size of each group. Teachers may want to limit groups to four or five students, which may require that they design more stations to keep the group sizes small. If teachers design more than four stations, it may be helpful to break the lesson up over the course of two days to avoid trying to cover too much in a single day or class period.

FIGURE 9.7 Designing a Station Rotation Lesson to Target Specific Skills

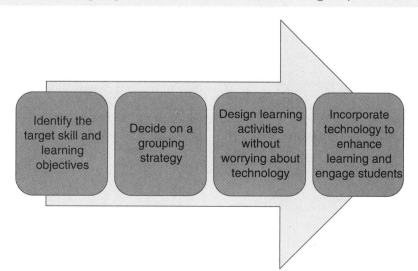

After identifying the target skill, selecting a grouping strategy, and deciding on the number of stations, you can design the learning activities and begin to think about how technology can be used in at least one unit to engage students, differentiate instruction, and/or personalize learning.

Laying out the stations visually is a helpful exercise when lesson planning for a small group rotation.

Vignette: Catlin Tucker, @Catlin_Tucker

The more I use the Station Rotation Model, the more I realize and appreciate how flexible it is. Instead of always approaching a Station Rotation lesson in the same way, I enjoy playing with this model to ensure it makes sense given the goals of the lesson.

I frequently use a variation of this model that I call Free Form Station Rotation. Students begin in one of three or four stations. When they are done with the task in that station, they are welcome to move on to the next station. I caution them to transition without disrupting those students still at work. I decided on this approach because I knew some students do not need as long as others to complete a given task. Instead, I want them to have the flexibility to work at their own pace and move when they are ready. It stunned me how focused and productive they were in each of the stations.

I've also experimented with what I call a One Stop Differentiated Station Rotation. In this lesson, students only visit one of the three or four stations, which have been set up with their ability level in mind. This strategy works well with reading because I have each station set up with reading materials aligned to that group's reading level. I also use this approach for writing stations where one group might need a lot of teacher support while the other stations require increasingly more independent work. The task at each station is geared toward the students in that particular station and there are necessary support materials available to aid students at different levels of mastery.

Right before finals this year, I designed Inspiration Stations. I could tell my students were totally fried from studying and needed to do something creative and fun. I designed three stations, each with a creative task, and allowed my students to select the station they wanted to visit. One group composed a song, while another group wrote a project proposal for a Donors Choose project they wanted funded. It was a fun way to approach stations that prioritized student choice and creativity.

Experimenting with the models is so much fun for me and adds some variety for the students. It's important that teachers not view the models as an endpoint, but rather a beginning with limitless opportunities.

What Are Some of the Challenges Associated With the Station Rotation Model?

As with any teaching style or strategy, there are also challenges associated with using the Station Rotation Model. Figure 9.8 identifies specific challenges associated with using this model and provides potential solutions to address common challenges.

FIGURE 9.8 Creative Solutions to Meet the Challenges of Using the Station Rotation Model

	CHALLENGES	SOLUTIONS
Access to Technology	Teachers must have access to technology for at least one learning station. It's ideal if the online learning station has enough devices for each student in that rotation.	Teachers working in low-tech schools or classrooms can maximize a handful of devices for this model. Elementary teachers may want to join Donors Choose to get funding for a few devices, or contact local computer recycling programs to ask about classroom donations. Secondary teachers working in a school with a wireless infrastructure that can support devices can leverage student devices (BYOD) to make this model work.
Cost of Adaptive Software	Adaptive software can be expensive for schools with limited budgets.	There are a growing number of free education tools and programs available online that allow for individualized practice (e.g., Khan Academy, NoRedInk, or Vocabulary.com).
Large Class Sizes	The larger the class size, the more challenging it is to keep groups small enough to ensure students stay focused and productive.	Teachers with larger class sizes may need to design more stations and rotate students through them over a few days to keep the number of students in each group low.
Lesson Planning	If the parts of a Station Rotation lesson build on each other, then students need to progress through the various activities in a particular order, which can be tricky to set up.	Teachers may need to plan lessons over a series of days with just one station building on the previous day's work, and allow students to progress through a series of steps.

(Continued)

FIGURE 9.8 (Continued)

	CHALLENGES	SOLUTIONS
Classroom Size and Furniture	The size of the classroom and the furniture available can also be an obstacle that makes moving around the room more difficult.	Investing in furniture that is lightweight, easy to move, and lends itself to collaboration can address this concern.
Facilitation and Classroom Management	Facilitating multiple learning stations, fielding questions, and keeping students on task may be challenging for a single teacher.	Teacher assistants, older students, and parent volunteers can help run additional stations, answer questions, provide support, and reinforce behavior expectations. At the secondary level, students with demonstrated mastery of a particular skill can also provide support to their peers. It's also important to help students build greater ownership in their learning.
Wide Range of Skills and/or Language Proficiencies	A class with a wide range of skill sets and/or language proficiencies may require more support when moving through stations.	Teachers can record short video tutorials or design dynamic Google Documents with clear explanations, screenshots, links, etc. so that each station provides students with additional instructions, explanations, and/or support.

Logistical Concerns

The following are questions to consider when designing a Station Rotation Model lesson:

- How should you group your students?

- How can you make sure students know the objectives of the activity?

- What do you do with students who finish a task before it's time to rotate?

- How do students know when and where to move around the room?

- What is the teacher's role during a Station Rotation lesson?

How to Group Your Students?

Teachers can group students by ability level so that a one-on-one or small group station with the teacher targets that group's ability level. However, heterogeneous groups can allow for a dynamic group collaboration station because students of different strengths and ability levels can work together to solve problems and learn. Alternatively, teachers can allow students to drive the creation of the groups by surveying them at the start of the year, or at the start of a unit to find out how they'd prefer to be grouped, what they feel their strengths are in a group dynamic, or how they prefer to learn.

There are benefits and drawbacks to any grouping strategy. The learning objectives and the activity itself should be the driving factors when deciding on the best grouping strategy for a given lesson. It's important that groups of students do not perceive themselves as the "smart" or "dumb" group. This can be avoided if teachers regularly change the groupings of students depending on the goals of each lesson. Figure 9.9 highlights different group strategies.

FIGURE 9.9 Grouping Strategies Explained

TYPE OF GROUPING STRATEGY	REASON FOR SELECTING THIS STRATEGY
Skill Level/Level of Mastery	This makes it possible to differentiate the learning at each station to challenge groups of students at their current ability level.
Interests and Passions	If group work allows students the autonomy to make decisions about what they want to work on or how to approach a project, then grouping by common interests and passions can be highly effective.
Grit, Motivation, and Drive	Gauging a student's "grit," motivation, and drive as a learner is important when forming groups, especially if those groups need to tackle a complex task.
Student Selected Groups	If students are working on a large-scale assignment that may require communication and collaboration both inside and outside of the classroom, they may be more excited and motivated to complete the work if they are in groups with students they enjoy and have formed positive relationships with already.
Strengths in a Group Dynamic	Students tend to gravitate toward particular roles in a group (e.g., natural leader, presenter, creator, etc.), so mixing up students to ensure that you have complementary dynamics in each group helps students help each other and be more successful.

Grouping Strategies

Teachers can group students in a variety of different ways depending on the learning goals or intended outcomes of a lesson. Figure 9.9 highlights some examples of grouping strategies and the reasons to select that strategy for a given activity. As teachers become more proficient in their blended practice, groupings of students can become a truly dynamic process—where on a weekly or even daily basis, teachers adjust groupings based on goals and needs.

How to Make Sure Students Know the Objectives of the Activity?

Many teachers are tempted to frontload a Station Rotation lesson by explaining the activity and objectives of each station to the entire class. Unfortunately, this sucks up valuable class time and as soon as students go to their first station, most will immediately ask, "What are we supposed to do?" This is incredibly frustrating for teachers, so it's worth exploring other strategies for outlining the tasks and objectives at each station. These strategies can save time and encourage students to take responsibility for their learning.

Teachers can

- print typed explanations and objectives for each of the stations that do not require technology. Then students can read through the directions and clarify questions as a group before they begin working. It may be helpful to add boxes for students to check as they progress through a multistep activity. The act of checking boxes as they complete tasks minimizes the chance that groups they skip important steps;

- create a Google Document with directions, images, screenshots, and links for each of the stations that require technology. These interactive multimedia documents are easy to share with students and connect them with all of the online resources they need to complete the task;

- record a video explanation of the instructions and objectives. Students can scan a quick response (QR) code that takes them to an online video tutorial, or teachers can share a video via Google Drive for students to access. Elementary teachers with access to devices like iPads can put one device at each station with the video explanation. This allows even young students with limited reading skills to complete tasks without the teacher present at the station; and finally

- use the Flipped Classroom Model to frontload a lesson. The night before a Station Rotation lesson, ask students to watch and take notes on a short video introducing the instructions and objectives for each station. This approach is better for older students and saves time if class periods are short. If teachers use this strategy, students should take notes on the video and those then serve as directions in the classroom.

What to Do With Students Who Finish a Task Before It's Time to Rotate?

It's important to anticipate and plan for those students who move more quickly through material. These students may complete the work at a station before it's time to rotate, so teachers must have a strategy to keep these kids engaged after they complete the work in their station. If there is nothing for them to do once they've completed their work, it's likely they will distract other members of the group who are still working. There are several strategies a teacher can use to keep those students engaged, so they are not tempted to distract their peers.

- Build "Next Steps" into each activity. These are additional activities that build on the work done at that station which push stronger students to think more deeply about the topic.

- Designate a part of the room where students can go to read silently, work on an art project, or get ahead on assignments for other classes.

- Ask those students who finish early to assist other members of their group or other groups. Often these students can be a fantastic support system for their peers. It's important that they know their role is similar to that of a tutor.

How Do Students Know When and Where to Move Around the Room?

Transitioning from station to station can be time consuming. It's crucial that teachers employ a consistent "cue" that lets students know when to move from one station to the next. Teachers may want to use a visual cue or an auditory cue depending on the activities taking place in the classroom.

Visual Cue Visual cues are best if students are working on a computer with headphones, and therefore may not hear the auditory cue. Teachers can cue a station change by turning the lights on and off a set number of times. Teachers can also project a timer with a countdown on the board so students can keep track of how much time they have to accomplish a task.

Auditory Cue If students are not wearing headphones, teachers can cue a station change with a chime, bell, or music.

Consistency is the most important aspect of using a cue. Students must know exactly what to do when they encounter the cue. There should be clear expectations for wrapping up work and moving to the next station when students see or hear the cue. The more accustomed students are to the routine, the more efficiently they will move around the room.

WHAT IS THE TEACHER'S ROLE
DURING A STATION ROTATION LESSON?

Although it's tempting to use the time students are on computers to lesson plan or grade, it's important that teachers stay engaged with their students and the lesson. One of the biggest benefits to using this model is the time it creates for teachers to work individually or with small groups of students to provide more personalized instruction, feedback, and support.

The job of the teacher during a Station Rotation varies. If the teacher is leading a station, then they are engaging with that group explaining concepts, modeling processes, and providing feedback. If the teacher is not leading a station, then he or she should circulate around the room to make sure groups understand the tasks, answer questions, work with groups that are struggling, or work one-on-one with students who need additional support. As the teacher circulates, he or she can also make some informal assessments to gauge understanding and identify students who are struggling. As a result, teachers will have a better sense of where each student is on his or her journey toward mastering particular skills. When students move lockstep through a uniform lesson, it is harder to identify which students are thriving and which students need additional scaffolding and support.

WRAPPING IT UP

In the Station Rotation Model, students rotate through learning stations with at least one station dedicated to online learning.

The Station Rotation Model creates smaller learning communities within the larger classroom; allows for more individualized and personalized instruction, affords opportunities to work with web tools and adaptive software that customizes to each individual learner; and offers exposure to a variety of activities that appeal to different learning modalities.

Despite the benefits of using this model, teachers shifting from a traditional teaching model to a Station Rotation Model need support from both teacher trailblazers and school leaders. Teacher trailblazers can use their expertise to model strong blended lessons and provide coaching and feedback to teachers just getting started; leaders can arrange for professional development, facilitate peer mentoring on campus, and ensure teachers have the technology necessary to employ this model.

BOOK STUDY QUESTIONS

1. What are the biggest benefits and/or challenges to using the Station Rotation Model? Are there any challenges or obstacles you are concerned with that were not addressed in this chapter? If so, what are they and how can you overcome these challenges?

2. What is your current access to technology? How does this impact your approach to using the Station Rotation Model? If your access to technology is limited, how can you make this model work with what you have?

3. If you are a teacher, is there any additional support you need in terms of the Links to Leadership section of this chapter? How can teacher trailblazers and leaders help to support you as you employ the Station Rotation Model? How can you make sure you get the support you need?

4. What new classroom management strategies do you need to employ to ensure the Station Rotation Model is successful? What new routines can you implement and practice with students to make the transition to a Station Rotation Model smoother?

5. Take one of your lessons and "go horizontal." What would a traditional lesson look like if you broke the individual tasks into stations? Does this make it easier to conceptualize a lesson? What is challenging about shifting from a traditional lesson to a Station Rotation lesson?

CHAPTER 10

Whole Group Rotation: A Modern Spin on the Lab Rotation

Learning should look like a bunch of people gathering new information. They should look engaged.

—George Payne, 7th Grade

WHAT IS THE WHOLE GROUP ROTATION?

The Whole Group Rotation is a modern spin on the old Lab Rotation Model. The Clayton Christensen Institute (2015) defines the Lab Rotation Model "as a course or subject in which students rotate to a computer lab for the online learning station" (Clayton Christensen, 2015, p. 1). However, Bring Your Own Device (BYOD) policies, 1:1 initiatives, and transportable technology in schools (e.g., iPad or Chromebook carts) are becoming more common, so the Whole Group Rotation allows teachers to rotate an entire class through a series of online and offline activities while remaining in a single classroom.

As schools continue to put devices in their students' hands, teachers will find that they can often transition from whole group instruction to practice on the computers without leaving their classroom. Many schools no longer need to adjust personnel or redesign facility use to employ the Lab Rotation Model because they have the technology available to allow students to remain in a single room for a given class. Instead of moving physically around a campus, the students simply rotate as a group between offline and online learning activities using the devices available to them in the classroom.

This chapter

- highlights the benefits of the Whole Group Rotation Model;
- provides strategies for designing Whole Group Rotation lessons;

- shares example lessons and a drag-and-drop lesson template to help teachers conceptualize a Whole Group Rotation Lesson;

- presents creative solutions to meet the challenges of using the Whole Group Rotation Model; and

- identifies logistical concerns teachers should consider.

Schools can look to implement the Whole Group Rotation Model in either Phase 1 or Phase 2 of the *Blended Learning Roadmap*. The Whole Group Rotation Model may provide a more incremental Phase 1 option for middle and high schools transitioning from a whole group, direct instruction model, while it may make sense in Phase 2 for elementary teachers who rely more on learning centers and less on whole group instruction.

WHAT ARE THE BENEFITS OF THE WHOLE GROUP ROTATION?

The Whole Group Rotation can serve as a transitional step for teachers shifting from a traditional whole group instruction to a Rotation Model. This approach may be more manageable for teachers beginning to explore blended learning because the class is moving through the same activity or task together instead of having multiple groups working on different tasks. The flow of the lesson also mirrors the lesson progression for a traditional class.

There are specific benefits of using Whole Group Rotation as opposed to the Station Rotation Model. A Whole Group Rotation

- weaves online elements into the whole group setting allowing students to control the pace and path of their learning;

- eliminates the need to move students around the room to different stations; and

- creates time and space for the teacher to work with individual students.

 Unlike traditional teaching where classes move lockstep through instruction and activities, the Whole Group Rotation uses online learning components to allow students the opportunity to control the pace and path of their own learning. For example, a teacher can design an online activity, such as a research task or a digital reading assignment, and students may work at different rates making their way through the content or activity to improve their comprehension and ability to apply that information. Additionally, teachers can use a range of online tools for practice that allow for a degree of personalization. That isn't possible with an offline lesson where every member of the class moves through a one-size-fits-all lesson. In a traditional lesson, the task may be too challenging for some students, but too easy for others. This is where adaptive learning technology is particularly important.

FIGURE 10.1   Specific Benefits of Whole Group Rotation

Weaves Online Elements Into the Whole Group Setting	• Online learning activities can be tailored to challenge individual students at their ability level. • Online elements allow students the opportunity to control both the pace and path of their learning.
Eliminates the Need to Move Around the Room	• There is less movement around the room, which saves time. • If students are not physically moving from place to place, it's easier to keep materials organized. • It may also be easier to manage a boisterous class if students do not change physical locations.
Creates Time and Space to Work With Individual Students	• Teachers can provide more scaffolding and support for struggling students and/or students with various language proficiencies. • Teachers can conference with students to review their work and discuss learning goals. • Teachers can more effectively gauge comprehension and mastery.

EdSurge, an educational technology company (2015), points out that the word "adaptive" is a buzzword used by a wide range of online products. However, it broadly states that "adaptive learning is an education technology that can respond to a student's interactions in real-time by automatically providing the student with individual support." EdSurge differentiates between adaptive content, adaptive assessment, and adaptive sequence. Adaptive content provides feedback based on the student's individual performance and "the tools provide materials to review the relevant skill." Adaptive assessments are tools "that change the questions a student sees based on his or her response to the previous question." And adaptive sequences are tools that collect and analyze "data to automatically change what a student sees next; from the order of skills . . . to the type of content a student receives" (Edsurge, 2016, p.1). (For more on Digital Curriculum, check out Chapter 6). Adaptive learning tools can be used during online activities in a Whole Group Rotation to personalize practice and assessment for each student.

When every student is working on a device during the online learning activities, it is an ideal time for the teachers to work individually with students. This time is invaluable because it allows the teacher to conference one-on-one with students about their progress, provide individual tutoring and support, and gauge individual student progress. Combined with the individual student data collected by adaptive learning tools and software, these one-on-one moments with students allow teachers to form a complete picture of where each child is in his or her learning.

Figure 10.2 depicts a generic Whole Group Rotation lesson. Students begin as a group with teacher-led instruction or work in small collaborative groups on the same learning activity. Then the entire group rotates to work on

FIGURE 10.2 Example of a Whole Group Rotation

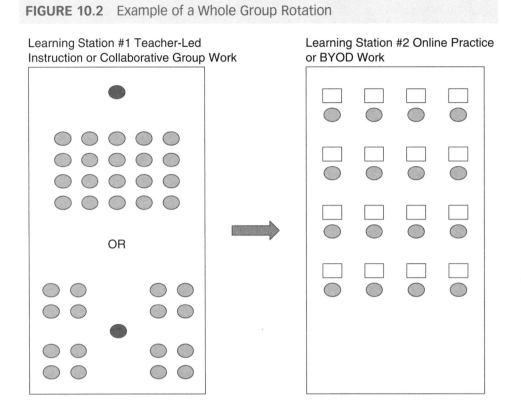

Learning Station #1 Teacher-Led Instruction or Collaborative Group Work

OR

Learning Station #2 Online Practice or BYOD Work

devices using online tools, accessing digital curriculum, or practicing skills with adaptive software. Depending on the length of the class period, students may move through several online and offline activities. There isn't an optimal number of activities. The number of activities depends entirely on time constraints, lesson objectives, and/or the pace at which your classes progress through activities.

DESIGNING A WHOLE GROUP ROTATION LESSON

Secondary teachers designing a Whole Group Rotation lesson learn that it is similar to designing a traditional lesson because the agenda flows linearly from one task to the next. Because the entire class is moving through the same online and offline tasks, the most challenging aspect of planning a Whole Group Rotation lesson is deciding how to use the technology to enhance the lesson objectives. Teachers need to explore web tools, online resources and/or adaptive technology to ensure the online components allow students the opportunity to pace their own learning, and whenever possible take their own path. This ensures that the time spent online is most effective.

Teachers can begin designing a Whole Group Rotation lesson by identifying the skills and objectives of the lesson, and then decide how many learning activities they have time to rotate their class through in a given day or period. Elementary teachers may have enough time to rotate students through several online and offline tasks in a day, but secondary teachers may only have time for two learning activities.

Once a teacher decides on the number of activities and the length of time needed for each, they can begin to work on the objectives and the materials for each activity. At this point, teachers should decide how to use technology during the online components of the lesson to enhance learning and offer a degree of personalization.

Figure 10.3 lays out a progression of items to consider as teachers plan a Whole Group Rotation lesson.

FIGURE 10.3 Planning a Whole Group Rotation Lesson

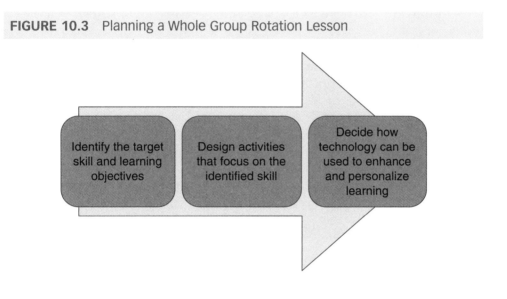

Catlin: It's important to note that a teacher might use a combination of strategies and blended learning models. I frequently shift between Station Rotation and Whole Group Rotation depending on my access to technology and the lesson objectives. If I am relying solely on the devices my students bring to class, then I'll design a Station Rotation Model to maximize the limited technology at our disposal. That also impacts the types of online stations I design since my students are working on a variety of devices and may not have access to specific apps or online programs. If I am able to secure a Chromebook cart for the day, then I might design a Whole Group Rotation so all of my students can work online simultaneously using specific programs.

Teachers want to use the best blended learning model for the specific lesson they are designing. As teachers try out different models, they may find that some work better for specific tasks. Teachers should feel free to mix and match as needed.

WHOLE GROUP ROTATION: SAMPLE LESSONS

One trap many teachers fall into when transitioning to blended learning is to assume that there is one correct way to plan and execute a lesson. The opposite is true. There are myriad approaches to designing a blended lesson, so I've included three examples of Whole Group Rotation Lessons in Figures 10.4, 10.5, and 10.6. Each lesson targets a specific subject area and combines a variety of online and face-to-face activities to enhance the quality of learning. The online components are designed to allow students to pace their own learning, collaborate with their peers, or practice with adaptive technology.

In the example lessons below, it's important to note the variety of activities. There isn't one correct way to design a Whole Group Rotation lesson. The lesson may begin with a modeling, inquiry, video explanation/demonstration, or crowdsourcing activity, which can be either teacher led or student led. The whole group activities vary between collaborative problem solving, science labs, and small group discussions. The online activities include individual practice with adaptive software like Khan Academy, and collaborative work online using cloud-based productivity tools like Google Apps. It's important for educators to pair each activity with the best learning medium for that activity to ensure that students have the opportunity to pace their own learning and work with peers to problem solve as needed.

FIGURE 10.4 Whole Group Rotation: Math Lesson

SAMPLE MATH LESSON

Introduction: Explanation and Modeling

Introduce a concept and model solving a problem (10 min)

Whole Group Activity: Collaborative Problem Solving

Students work collaboratively to solve a practice problem (15 min)

- Break students into groups of three to four.
- Provide each group with the same problem.
- Allow time for groups to work collaboratively drawing on the information from the start of the lesson to solve the problem.
- Ask one member of the group with a device to take a picture of the solution and post it to a shared Padlet Wall (Padlet.com).
- Once all pictures are posted, project the Padlet Wall and talk through the various solutions as a class.

Online Learning Activity: Individual Practice

Individual work on devices using adaptive technology to personalize practice: Khan Academy, TenMarks, or Redbird Math (20 min)

Concluding Activity

Exit ticket—paper or online (5 min)

FIGURE 10.5   Whole Group Rotation: Science Lesson

SAMPLE SCIENCE LESSON

Introduction: Online Learning with an In-Class Flip

Video lecture or demonstration (10 min)

- Students watch a video and take notes individually.

Whole Group Activity: Science Lab (30 min)

Students work in lab groups to complete an experiment using information from the video.

- As they work, students document their work with mobile devices–taking pictures, recording short videos, and/or capturing audio clips.
- After completing the experiment, individual groups discuss results.

Online Activity: Collaborative Lab Report with Google Documents

- Each group works collaboratively on a shared Google Document to write a lab report detailing their work and results.
- Students reference their documentation and use images, videos, and audio to ensure their writing is detailed and accurate.

Note: This collaborative writing activity likely needs to continue for homework.

FIGURE 10.6   Whole Group Rotation: History Lesson

SAMPLE HISTORY LESSON

Introduction: Crowdsource Information on a Topic (15 min)

- Break students into small groups of three to four.
- Give them a specific topic to research.
- Allow students time to research on devices and discuss their findings.
- Ask each group to share the information they found by writing it on the board, or posting it online to a shared blog, Padlet Wall, or wikispace.
- As a class, review the information correcting inaccurate information, building on information shared, and answering any questions that come up.

Online Activity: Video or Documentary (10–15 min)

Students watch a video explaining in more detail the topic they crowdsourced.

Note: History.com, Khan Academy, and both of the Youtube Channel videos: "The Smithsonian Is" and "CrashCourse" are excellent places to grab videos on history.

- Students take notes as they watch the video.

(Continued)

FIGURE 10.6   (Continued)

Whole Group Activity: Small Group Discussions (10 min)

Ask students to discuss the information from the crowdsourcing activity and video.

- Count students off by four. Ask all of the ones to go to one corner of the room, all twos go to another corner of the room, and so on.
- Each group should sit in a circle to discuss the information they found during research and learned during the video.
  - ○ What was most interesting?
  - ○ Was anything unclear?
  - ○ Do you have any questions after researching and watching the video?

Concluding Activity

Exit ticket—paper or online (5 min)

"Crowdsourcing" is a term that was coined by Jeff Howe and first appeared in an article he wrote for Wired Magazine in 2006. Howe defines crowdsourcing as "the act of taking a job traditionally performed by a designated agent (usually an employee) and outsourcing it to an undefined, generally large group of people in the form of an open call" (Crowdsourcing, 2006, p. 1). Instead of the teacher serving as the single source of information in a classroom, the class (or crowd) generates information via research. This simple strategy radically changes the flow of information in a classroom. Instead of a one-way flow of information from teacher to student, all members of the class community are actively engaged in finding and sharing information.

WHOLE GROUP ROTATION: DRAG-AND-DROP LESSON TEMPLATE

The drag-and-drop lesson template, pictured in Figure 10.7, provides a flexible template teachers can copy and customize. Teachers can plan a lesson by dragging the activities into the specific order that works for a given lesson. The text can also be tailored for each specific lesson.

Some teachers may begin with an online warm-up or review activity, then transition to a whole group exercise and conclude with individualized practice on devices. While others may want to begin with whole group instruction to introduce a concept, allow students to work collaboratively in groups, and then transition to online work. The individual lesson dictates the approach to blending face-to-face interactions with online components.

To use the drag-and-drop lesson design template, follow these five steps:

1. Log into your Google account.

2. Go to this link: bit.ly/dragdroplesson

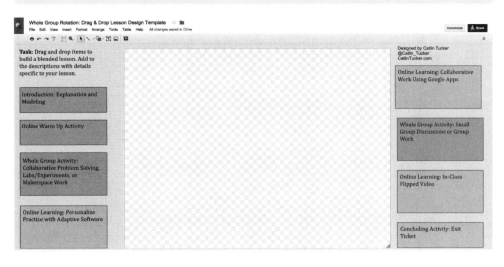

3. Click "File" on the Google Drawing and select "Make a copy."

4. Give your copy a name and it automatically saves in your Google Drive.

5. Once saved, you can make as many copies as you like and customize each, work collaboratively with colleagues, and easily share your lesson plans.

WHAT ARE SOME OF THE CHALLENGES ASSOCIATED WITH THE WHOLE GROUP ROTATION?

Even though the Whole Group Rotation does not radically change the way a teacher designs a lesson, it does present some challenges. Figure 10.8 identifies specific challenges associated with using the Whole Group Rotation and provides some potential solutions to address common problems.

The Whole Group Rotation does require that teachers have enough devices for each student so that everyone can access the online learning activity at the same time. This can be accomplished if teachers are in a 1:1 environment or have easy access to a computer lab or mobile cart with devices. In a 1:1 environment, students can work on their laptops, Chromebooks, or devices when they transition from whole group instruction into the practice phase of the lesson.

FIGURE 10.8 Creative Solutions to Meet the Challenges of Using the Whole Group Rotation

CHALLENGES	SOLUTIONS
Managing Devices	When devices are on every desk, they can be a distraction if teachers do not have a clear management strategy for minimizing distractions during offline activities.	Teachers can establish clear routines around using devices at the start of the year. Students using iPads or hand-held devices, like smartphones, can put their devices volume off and screen down to minimize the chance that notifications distract them during offline activities. Students using laptops or Chromebooks can completely close their devices or tilt their screens to a 45° angle so the content on the screen is not visible.
Wide Range of Skills and/or Language Proficiencies	A class with a wide range of skill sets and/or language proficiencies may have students who require more support during particular activities.	Teachers can use the online activity time to work individually with students who are struggling. If a teacher is unable to work directly with a student, they may ask a strong student in the class to step in as peer tutor. It's also helpful to anticipate questions and have support resources (e.g., links to online video tutorials) ready to share with students who need them.
Technology and Infrastructure	Whenever teachers use technology or rely on Wi-Fi for lessons, there is the danger that the technology or Wi-Fi might not work properly.	It's important to have an offline backup plan. Educators using technology must be flexible and understand that technology hiccups happen. It's important to adapt lessons in the moment and model what it looks like to troubleshoot technology issues and problems for students.
Timing and Pacing	The time it takes students to complete activities, especially online learning elements, may vary.	If students move through online activities at different rates, it's important to have "next steps," or additional activities in place so they can continue working without distracting peers. Online elements can be the final section of the lesson, so students who need more time can continue working outside of class.

LINKS TO LEADERSHIP:
ACCESS TO TECHNOLOGY

- Teachers interested in using a Whole Group Rotation need access to technology for every student if they are all working online at the same time. Leaders need to decide on a strategy for putting technology into their students' hands. The first question a school leader must consider is the question of whether or not there is adequate financial resources to purchase devices. If so, what type of devices are within your budget (iPads, Chromebooks, laptops)?

- Will you purchase one type of device for every student or will teachers/departments have access to carts with the device of their choice?

- How will you engage teachers in a conversation about the best devices for their grade level and/or subject area? (For more on selecting the right devices, check out Chapter 5: Devices and Digital Tools.)

If there is no budget for hardware, leaders need to be more creative in their approach.

- Can the campus infrastructure support a bring your own devices (BYOD) policy? If not, is there money to invest in infrastructure?

- If you decide to embrace a BYOD policy as a school or district, how will you communicate with parents? You'll need to articulate the value of devices and technology in the classroom to secure parent buy-in. It's also important to consider purchasing devices to have on hand for those students without a personal device.

- Are there computer labs available for teachers to rotate in and out of during the school day? How will administration handle the scheduling of computer lab time to ensure it is equitable?

Depending on the length of the class period, teachers can include a small group collaborative activity that complements the whole group instruction and online learning activity. Teachers can break the class into smaller groups and each group can work on the same task. This builds in time for students to work together in small collaborative groups to problem solve, research, and apply what they've learned. It also allows time for the teacher to circulate around the room providing individualized feedback and support. This is a key benefit of the Rotation Model, so it's crucial that teachers use the time students are working individually on computers to work one-on-one with students who are struggling or need additional support.

It's also important to remember that offline activities are not limited to direct instruction. This time can be used to allow students to discuss, problem solve, collaborate, and create. Teachers can use offline time for kinesthetic learning activities using the Makerspace Model. The more creative a teacher is when planning these lessons, the more effective they'll be!

LOGISTICAL CONCERNS

The following are questions a teacher considers when designing a Whole Group Rotation Model lesson:

- How can I make sure students are on task during online work?
- How can I make time to work one-on-one with students?

How can I make sure students are on task during online work?

Classroom management software programs, like SoftLINK for Chromebooks or Faronics Insight, allow teachers to monitor their students' computer screens and eliminate distractions by limiting student access to websites and applications. These programs help to keep students on task and make monitoring student work and progress more manageable for the teacher.

In addition to classroom management software programs, there are classroom management tools like Class Dojo that help teachers to reinforce positive behaviors in the class during both online and offline work. Class Dojo is easy for teachers to use right from their smartphone or iPad. Teachers can customize the specific behaviors they want to reinforce and communicate directly with students and parents about performance in the classroom.

How can I make time to work one-on-one with students?

While students are working online, teachers can use that time to work one-on-one with students who need additional support or instruction. It's helpful to create a teacher-student workstation or area in the classroom where you can work one-on-one with students while still keeping an eye on the class as they work.

WRAPPING IT UP

The consequence of the growth of mobile devices, BYOD policies, 1:1 initiatives, and mobile technology carts on school campuses means that more teachers are blending online learning with face-to-face interactions using the Whole Group Rotation. Like the Station Rotation Model, students move through a series of online and offline activities. However, the Whole Group Rotation Model does not require students to physically move around the room to various stations. Instead, the class moves through a series of activities together, including at least one online learning activity where students can control the pace and potentially the path of their learning.

Although the Whole Group Rotation follows the same linear approach to lesson design as most secondary teachers already employ, there are still logistical concerns worth considering. Classroom management becomes important when students are working online. Teachers must establish routines and clear expectations to ensure work online does not distract from learning, but rather enhances it.

Traditional teachers shifting from one-size-fits-all offline lessons need support from both teacher trailblazers and school leaders. Teacher trailblazers can use their expertise to model strong blended lessons and provide coaching and feedback to teachers just getting started. Leaders should coordinate the technology needed to execute Whole Group Rotation, because this model works best when every child has access to a device. Leaders also need to support teachers with the necessary professional development, facilitate peer mentoring on campus, and ensure that teachers have the technology necessary to employ this model.

BOOK STUDY QUESTIONS

1. What do you feel are the biggest benefits and/or challenges of using Whole Group Rotation as compared to Station Rotation? Are there any challenges or obstacles that you are concerned with that were not addressed in this chapter? If so, what are they and how might you overcome these challenges?

2. Given your grade level, subject area, and access to technology, do you think you will more frequently use the Station Rotation or Whole Group Rotation? What might make one rotation model easier to use than another?

3. What is your current access to technology? How does this impact your approach to using the Whole Group Rotation? If your access to technology is limited, how can you make this model work with the technology you have?

4. If you are a teacher, is there any additional support you need in terms of the Links to Leadership section of this chapter? How can teacher trailblazers and leaders in leadership positions help to support you as you employ the Whole Group Rotation? How can you make sure you get the support you need?

5. What new classroom management strategies do you need to employ to ensure the Whole Group Rotation is successful? What new routines can you implement and practice with students to make a smooth transition to a Whole Group Rotation?

CHAPTER 11

The Flipped Classroom

Learning shouldn't look like one specific thing. It should revolve around that one student. My learning should look different from the person sitting next to me. Everyone learns differently. ONE way of learning won't fit everyone.

—Britney Hassett, 10th Grade

WHAT IS THE FLIPPED CLASSROOM?

The Flipped Classroom Model is a subcategory of the Rotation Model that allows a teacher in a traditional classroom setting to shift the transfer of information online and pull practice and application into the classroom.

Classically, the transfer of information occurred in the classroom via lecture or reading a text, and the practice and application phase of learning was assigned for homework. However, the benefit of this "flipped" inversion is that students are able to pace their learning online at home to improve comprehension and their ability to apply that information. The class time created by shifting instruction and lecture online is used to focus on the creative application of the information.

It's during the application phase of learning when most students struggle and need support. Unfortunately, students may not have parents at home who can help them apply the information they've been taught in class. Some parents work in the evenings, lack the subject area expertise, or speak a different language than the one in which work is presented. These factors can create barriers to success for students who struggle to apply information at home. When students work at home, isolated and alone, they do not have access to a subject area expert or a group of peers who can answer questions, re-explain concepts, and assist them if they are struggling.

If class time is used to allow students to apply what they have learned in cooperation with their peers, then the Flipped Classroom Model encourages collaboration, inquiry, and problem solving. When students attempt to apply information in the classroom, they are not doing it on their own. They have support from the teacher and a community of peers as they work. Because teachers are not standing at the front of the room talking, they can circulate around the room answering questions and lending support.

The beauty of the Flipped Classroom lies in the simple realization that instruction can take place in different mediums. Learning is no longer limited to a class period or a physical classroom. Teachers have the opportunity to match the instructional activity with the learning environment that makes the most sense.

This chapter

- highlights the benefits of the Flipped Classroom Model;

- provides strategies for designing a flipped lesson;

- shares example lessons with a reusable lesson template;

- explores how teachers can flip with different types of media—text, images, and video;

- explains the importance of flipping and engaging students online around the flipped content;

- reviews the steps required to produce and publish original video content;

- presents creative solutions to meet the challenges of using the Flipped Classroom Model; and

- examines how the Station Rotation Model and the Flipped Classroom Model can combine to bring all parts of the flipped lesson into the classroom.

Because of the shift in mindset and increased student ownership of the Flipped Classroom Model, it is aligned with Phase 2 or Phase 3 of the *Blended Learning Roadmap*.

WHAT ARE THE BENEFITS OF THE FLIPPED CLASSROOM?

The Flipped Classroom allows students the opportunity to control the pace of their learning, which is particularly helpful for students who struggle, need accommodations, or are not native English speakers. This inversion also creates more time for student-centered learning in the classroom, and affords teachers more opportunities for formative assessment.

When Catlin surveyed her 9th and 10th grade students with a Google Form at the end of first semester, she asked them if they preferred to watch videos or if they would prefer for her to present information in class. Of the eighty students who took the survey, only two said they preferred that she review information in class. Seventy-eight students said they preferred the flipped model. When asked to explain why they preferred one method to the other, she received the following responses:

"I liked the flipped classroom because I could go on at my own pace and not be rushed into doing work with limited time" (Ian, 9th grade).

"This learning approach was helpful because I was able to watch a video as many times as needed and pause it as much as I wanted. It helped a lot being able to go at my own pace and rewatch sections. It was helpful using class time to play with the words" (Gemma, 9th grade).

"Yes. I think one of the reasons I like this class is because I can pace myself. It helps the information stick into my head because we aren't just wasting time learning it in class, but we are actually applying what we learned in the classroom" (Alyssa, 10th grade).

DESIGNING A FLIPPED CLASSROOM LESSON

As educators embrace the Flipped Classroom, it is helpful to think about designing flipped lessons in three steps (see Figure 11.2). Planning a flipped lesson requires that teachers decide what happens in class and what happens online to ensure each part of the lesson flows seamlessly into the next. We suggest the following progression for a typical flipped lesson.

FIGURE 11.1 Specific Benefits of Using the Flipped Classroom

Encourages Self-Paced Learning	• Students can pause, rewind, or rewatch a video. • They can look up unfamiliar words, or do a Google search to better understand what they are reading or watching. • They have time to process and reflect on the information they are asked to read, view, or watch, making it easier for them to discuss and apply the information when they come to class.
Creates a Student-Centered Learning Environment	• Class time can be used to group students for collaborative activities that require them to discuss, collaborate, and apply information. • The focus is not on the teacher at the front of the room lecturing; instead, the focus is on the students working to apply information. • There's more time for students to work with information and concepts together in class where they can support and learn from one another.
Allows for More Formative Assessment	• The teacher can move around the room talking to students, checking for understanding and providing support. This helps the teacher to more effectively gauge comprehension. • The information collected as students work can be used to provide additional scaffolding for students who need it. Teachers can also design extension activities for those students who need to be challenged further.

FIGURE 11.2 Designing a Flipped Classroom Lesson

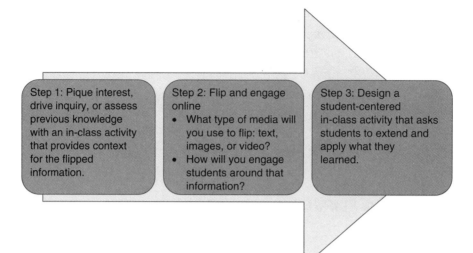

Step 1: Pique interest, drive inquiry, or assess previous knowledge with an in-class activity that provides context for the flipped information.

Step 2: Flip and engage online
- What type of media will you use to flip: text, images, or video?
- How will you engage students around that information?

Step 3: Design a student-centered in-class activity that asks students to extend and apply what they learned.

Step 1: Pique Interest, Drive Inquiry, or Assess Previous Knowledge

First, teachers must design an in-class activity to create context for the flipped information students are to engage with online. When planning the activity that precedes the flipped information, teachers can use several different strategies.

- Pique interest by asking a question, showing a video clip, or presenting students with a situation or problem to consider and discuss.

- Drive inquiry around a topic by asking students to generate questions.

- Gauge previous knowledge with a brainstorm activity.

- Encourage students to make predictions.

Step 2: Flip and Engage Online

Although the conversation about the flipped classroom tends to focus on the media used to transfer information, it's also important to consider how teachers can engage students around that online content and information to push them out of their passive roles as receivers of information into more active roles as learners.

Just as teachers want to engage students in the classroom, it's important to engage them online as well. If they are asked to do something with the information presented online, they are more likely to think critically about the information, thus improving retention. Because teachers are capitalizing on the student's connectivity at home to flip in the first place, it is a natural extension to consider how they can use that same connectivity to connect students around that information using asynchronous online discussions, an online tool like EdPuzzle, or collaborative tasks using Google Apps.

> Just as teachers want to engage students in the classroom, it's important to engage them online as well.

Teachers should consider the following questions when preparing the flipped part of their blended lesson:

- What information will you flip?
- What form of media is most effective in communicating that information?
- How will you engage students around that flipped content to encourage them to examine it critically about?

Step 3: Design Student-Centered Application Activities

Finally, teachers should use class time after students have seen the flipped content to get them working to apply that information. Because students are in a physical space together, it is ideal to use this time to allow them to work collaboratively to apply concepts. Teachers can capitalize on the collective intelligence of the students in the room for these activities. This student-centered approach encourages communication, inquiry, research, problem solving, and collaboration.

It's important to note that teachers who use the extra class time created to assign more worksheets in class will find it challenging to motivate students to complete homework in this model. However, if students come to class knowing the application and extension activities are likely to be student centered, collaborative, and creative there is more of an incentive to complete the work prior to class.

The template pictured in Figure 11.3 guides teachers through the process of planning their flipped lessons.

To use the flipped classroom lesson template above, follow these steps:

1. Log into your Google account.
2. Go to this link: bit.ly/flippedtemplate
3. Click "File" on the Google Document and select "Make a copy."
4. Give your copy a name and it will automatically save in your Google Drive.
5. Once saved, you can make as many copies as you like and customize each, work collaboratively with colleagues, and easily share your lesson plans with students, parents, or colleagues.

FIGURE 11.3 Flipped Classroom Lesson Template

Step 1: Inquiry and Exploration

Activity description:

What materials or tech tools do you need for this step?

Where does this step in the lesson take place (home, class, in stations)?

Step 2: Transfer Information and Engage

Activity description:

What materials or tech tools do you need for this step?

Where does this step in the lesson take place (home, class, in stations)?

How do you assess this step (if desired)?

Step 3: Extend and Apply

Activity description:

What materials or tech tools do you need for this step?

Where does this step in the lesson take place (home, class, in stations)?

How do you assess this step (if desired)?

@Catlin_Tucker

In English, I introduce fifteen SAT vocabulary words every other week. For years, I stood at the front of the classroom to present vocabulary words for students to copy into their notes. I projected the list with my transparency machine and went through each word in detail–pronouncing each word, unpacking complex definitions, and providing examples–as my students wrote down the words, parts of speech, and definitions.

Inevitably, there were students in the back of the room yelling, "Slow down, Tucker! I'm four words behind!" while students in the front row waited impatiently for me to continue. I was never able to please everyone because my students worked at different paces and processed information at different rates. Additionally, the students racing to catch up often made mistakes copying down the words and definitions. Those students who were absent missed the opportunity to hear the vocabulary instruction entirely and were forced to copy the words from a friend.

Reflecting on my practice as an educator, I realized my method for teaching vocabulary was not working. It took me twenty minutes to get through a given vocabulary list with each of my six classes. I was spending a whopping two hours of instructional time every other week going over vocabulary. My approach to vocabulary instruction was inefficient and ineffective for the majority of students. This realization inspired me to shift to the Flipped Classroom Model for vocabulary, and subsequently for writing and grammar instruction.

EXAMPLE OF A FLIPPED VOCABULARY LESSON

Below is the flipped vocabulary lesson Catlin Tucker uses with her 9th and 10th grade English students.

FIGURE 11.4 Example of Catlin's Flipped Vocabulary Lesson

Step 1: Inquiry and Exploration

Before my students watch their vocabulary video, I put them into small groups of three to four students. I give each group a sheet of paper that has all of their vocabulary words used in context.

What materials or tech tools do you need for this step?

I write 15 sentences using each vocabulary word in context and make copies—one for each group.

(Continued)

FIGURE 11.4 (Continued)

I underline their vocabulary words, so my students can identify their new vocabulary. At this point they have not been introduced to the words or definitions.

They work in their small groups of three to four to make predictions about what they think each word means based on how it is used in the sentence. This encourages them to determine or clarify the meaning of unknown words and phrases by using context clues and analyzing meaningful word parts, which is a key to success beyond high school.

Unfortunately, many students blow right past unfamiliar vocabulary when they read. Few stop to consider context clues or try to make an educated guess about the meaning of words they do not know. The objective of this step in our vocabulary practice is to train students to slow down and think critically about unfamiliar vocabulary. I hope my students begin to see sentences with unfamiliar vocabulary as a puzzle that can be solved given a closer look at the parts of the sentence. This anticipating activity serves to set the stage for the flipped content.

Where does this step in the lesson take place (home, class, in stations)?

The predictions take place in the classroom where students can work together in small groups to discuss the context clues in each sentence and make predictions.

How do you assess this step (if desired)?

I informally assess engagement as I walk around the room observing groups discussing the sentences and making predictions. The accuracy of the predictions is not as important as the quality of the conversations and level of engagement.

Step 2: Transfer Information and Engage

Once students have copied down the vocabulary, they write a narrative using ten of their fifteen vocabulary words. They post their narratives to an asynchronous discussion on Schoology. They know their narratives must communicate the meaning of the words they are using and demonstrate creativity, time, and effort.

Once students have posted their narratives, they read and reply to at least two other members of the class complimenting strong word use or stories, identifying incorrect word use and gently suggesting improvements, and asking questions. They can "like" the stories they really enjoyed, and then those students who received the most "likes" from peers

What materials or tech tools do you need for this step?

I design my vocabulary presentations using Google Slides. On one slide I write the word, part of speech, and definition. On the next slide I insert an image that I hope helps students remember the word. For example, if the word is "notorious," then I might use an image of Miley Cyrus. If the word is "ponder," I might use an image of a person sitting alone obviously in deep thought.

Once I design a multimedia vocabulary presentation, I record a screencast using Quicktime on my Mac laptop. After recording the screencast, I export it directly to YouTube.

are invited to read their stories to the class the next day.

This approach addresses several standards simultaneously. Students are learning new vocabulary, they are completing a piece of narrative writing, as well as publishing online and interacting with their peers using the internet.

I also create a Schoology discussion with a link to the YouTube video and directions for writing the narrative and responding to peers.

Where does this step in the lesson take place (home, class, in stations)?

Students watch the video and write their narratives using ten of the fifteen words at home.

How do you assess this step (if desired)?

I check that all students have their Cornell notes the next day in class. I also assess the quality of the students' narratives using a simple two point rubric attached to the Schoology discussion that assesses 1) how well the word use communicates meaning, and 2) the overall creativity of the narrative on a scale of one to four.

Step 3: Extend and Apply

When students return to class after watching the vocabulary video and writing their narratives, they complete a series of activities to get them working with the words.

First, students working in groups of three or four are asked to use their devices or the dictionaries and thesauri in our room to find a synonym and antonym for each word. This activity helps them to better understand word relationships.

Second, students review the words by playing Socrative Space Races, a game composed of multiple-choice questions that ask students to select the word that correctly completes the sentence. These "Space Races" allow groups or teams to compete against each other to see which group correctly answers the most questions.

Sometimes students publish their narratives by reading them aloud to the class or they play Word Sneak, a game Catlin adapted from Jimmy Fallon's *Tonight Show* to make vocabulary review more fun.

Check out Catlin's blog on Word Sneak—bit.ly/wordsneak

What materials or tech tools do you need for this step?

There is no setup required for the synonym and antonym search, but students need their devices and/or dictionaries and thesauri to look up words.

I prepare a vocabulary review game in Socrative to prepare for a Space Race activity.

If the students play Word Sneak, I preview examples of Jimmy Fallon playing with guests and select one to show students. Then I print out the vocabulary words and make copies for students to use when they play Word Sneak.

Where does this step in the lesson take place (home, class, in stations)?

Review activities take place in the classroom.

How do you assess this step (if desired)?

I visually check that all students have completed the synonym and antonym search.

I also informally assess engagement during the Word Sneak activity.

The formal assessment for vocabulary is the quiz students take after working with the words for a week and a half.

Our classroom is unlike any other. We do the rudimentary yet essential tasks at our homes, and return to school for more in-depth learning. For example, we learn our vocabulary by taking notes from a prerecorded video, and then secure our understanding of the words' meaning by discovering synonymous words and their antonyms. Later we create a narrative online, incorporating the current words into our unique stories, as well as providing constructive criticism of our peers' narratives. With this method, I and other members of our class can easily retain the introduced terminology and learn how to apply it in an inspired, imaginative, and grammatically correct way. Because of this innovative teaching method, which is painless to acclimate to, I am developing an exceedingly more colorful vocabulary that broadens my knowledge, and improves my writing skills, which will undoubtedly benefit me in the approaching prospect of college.

FLIPPING WITH DIFFERENT TYPES OF MEDIA

Often conversations about the Flipped Classroom are myopically focused on videos. This is concerning on two counts. First, videos are just one type of media a teacher can use to "flip" his or her instruction. Second, the videos (or whatever media you choose to use) are simply a vehicle for creating more time and space in the classroom that can be dedicated to creatively applying that information. The magic of the Flipped Classroom is not in the media you select, but rather in how you use your class time to engage students, encourage higher-order thinking, foster collaboration, assess student comprehension, and support those students who need additional help.

Flipping With Text

As more digital texts become available online, the opportunities to flip with online texts and engage students around those texts in a dynamic way. For example, teachers can link students to online articles and ask them to use an online annotation tool, like Diigo, to digitally highlight and take notes on what they are reading. Then, those notes can be shared directly with the teacher via a unique URL or an email.

Alternatively, teachers can use a dynamic online offering, like StudySync, to have students annotate texts, answer text dependent questions about the reading, and complete a wide range of written responses. This shifts reading from a passive to an active experience.

Figure 11.5 recommends online resources that teachers can use to flip their instruction with text.

FIGURE 11.5 Recommended Resources for Flipping With Text

ONLINE READING RESOURCE	URL	DESCRIPTION
StudySync	www.studysync.com	StudySync is a "cross-curricular, core literacy solution designed to advance reading, writing, critical thinking, speaking and listening skills." It has a growing collection of digital texts—literary, nonfiction, speeches—paired with "Think questions" and writing prompts. Students can listen to audio recordings of the text, digitally annotate with the built-in annotation tool, and provide anonymous peer feedback.
Newsela	https://newsela.com	A collection of nonfiction literature and current events offered at various Lexile levels to challenge readers at different reading levels. Texts are paired with Common Core aligned quizzes. The Pro version allows teachers to collect data on student progress.
Smithsonian Tween Tribune	http://tweentribune.com	TweenTribune is "a free online educational service offered by the Smithsonian for use by K–12 grade." Teachers and students that offers a range of articles written at four different Lexile levels. Students can leave comments on articles, and each article includes a three-question quiz.
CommonLit	www.commonlit.org	CommonLit is a collection of free fiction and nonfiction texts for classrooms. Texts are arranged thematically and can be printed or read online. Each text includes text dependent questions and discussion prompts.
Library of Congress	www.loc.gov	The Library of Congress is "the nation's oldest federal cultural institution, and it serves as the research arm of Congress," which houses a collection of primary and secondary sources, such as print, audio, and video.
ReadWorks.org	www.readworks.org	ReadWorks provides "research-based units, lessons, and authentic, leveled nonfiction and literary passages directly to educators online, for free, to be shared broadly."
Storyline Online	www.storylineonline.net	The SAG-AFTRA Foundation records well-known actors reading children's books and makes graphically dynamic videos so that children around the world can be read to with just the click of a Storyline Online video book image.

Flipping With Images

Students today are choosing to engage with the world in increasingly visual ways. They share pictures and videos with photo sharing apps, like Instagram, Snapchat, and Vine. This affinity for all things visual requires that educators teach students to look critically at images, photographs, artwork, graphs, flowcharts, maps, and infographics to draw conclusions about those images.

If you are wondering . . . can I really flip my class with photos or images? The answer is "Yes." If students have time to sit and appreciate the nuances of an image or graph and think deeply about the details, they can learn more from that experience than if data is projected for three minutes while a teacher talks about it.

In a traditional classroom setting, there is not enough time for students to control the pace of their learning, even if they are simply looking at an image. This fact serves as a clear benefit to moving information online. For example, consider a world history teacher who presents a painting and asks his students to analyze the different aspects of the painting—subject, lines, shapes, form, texture—to identify the historical time period and region where the students believe it was produced. If the image is presented online, students have time to evaluate the various elements of the painting then articulate an explanation supporting their position. If that teacher embeds the artwork into an asynchronous discussion, then students have time to observe, analyze, *and* discuss the piece with their peers, which consistently yields more meaningful learning.

Figure 11.6 recommends online resources teachers can use to flip their instruction with images and artwork.

FIGURE 11.6   Recommended Resources for Flipping With Images

IMAGE RESOURCE	URL	DESCRIPTION
MoMA	www.moma.org	The official website of the Museum of Modern Art.
Louvre	www.louvre.fr/en	The official website of the Louvre Museum.
National Gallery of Art	www.nga.gov/content/ngaweb.html	The official website of the National Gallery of Art.
Natural History Museum	www.mnh.si.edu/panoramas	A virtual tour of the Smithsonian National Museum of Natural History.
Google Art Project	www.google.com/culturalinstitute/project/art-project	Virtual collections from around the world with artworks photographed in high resolution. Teachers can create and share collections of masterpieces.

There are a growing number of virtual museum tours that can be used to flip with artwork. For example, many of the most famous art galleries around the world offer virtual tours for online visitors. The Louvre in Paris, the Smithsonian in Washington D.C., and the Museum of Modern Art (MoMA) in New York City all have dynamic virtual tours that can be used to flip and engage kids online with images and artwork.

Flipping With Video

This is the classic flip. Most teachers who have heard of the flipped classroom have heard about flipping with video. Although this approach, made popular by chemistry teachers Jonathan Bergmann and Aaron Sams, is the most popular way to flip instruction, it does pose some challenges for educators. Teachers may be concerned about the time it takes to create flipped content, or they may not have easy access to the technology or software needed to create flipped videos. It's important to note that while many teachers prefer to create their own video content, there are tons of online resources where teachers can capture video content to use with students.

TED-Ed, a free educational website for teachers and learners offered by TED (Technology, Entertainment, Design), has a growing collection of ready-to-use virtual lessons wrapped around high quality video content. Users can flip a TED-Ed lesson and use it as is, or they can edit the lesson and customize it for their students.

Figure 11.7 recommends online resources teachers can use to flip their instruction with video content.

Flip AND Engage

Often the homework described in the Flipped Classroom Model only engages the lower-level thinking skills described in Bloom's Taxonomy—remembering and understanding. The application, analysis, evaluation, and creation are rarely engaged at home. There is an opportunity to get students thinking at a higher level at home if teachers pair content with activities that require them to think critically about what they have read or viewed. The important element is to ask students to do something with the information and connect students online outside of class so they have a support network of peers to ask questions, share ideas with, and learn from.

Instead of simply presenting students with a video to watch, teachers can build an entire lesson around that video with tools like TED-Ed or EdPuzzle, which enable the ability to ask questions about the video content to keep students attentive and engaged while informally assessing their comprehension. Similarly, teachers can embed a complex graph, map, or infographic into an

FIGURE 11.7 Recommended Resources for Flipping With Videos

VIDEO RESOURCE	URL	DESCRIPTION
TED-Ed	http://ed.ted.com	TED-Ed is "a free educational website for teachers and learners. They are a global and interdisciplinary initiative with a commitment to creating lessons worth sharing."
Khan Academy	www.khanacademy.org	Khan Academy "offers practice exercises, instructional videos, and a personalized learning dashboard that empower learners to study at their own pace in and outside of the classroom."
History.com	www.history.com	History.com offers a range of historical information, including famous speeches, historical video footage, and interviews with influential people.
PBS LearningMedia	www.pbslearningmedia.org	PBS LearningMedia "builds on the strength of public media and is designed to improve teacher effectiveness and student achievement. Resources are aligned to Common Core and national standards and include videos and interactives, as well as audio, documents, and in-depth lesson plans."

LINKS TO LEADERSHIP: ACCESS TO TECHNOLOGY

The resources in Figure 11.7 are just a few examples of great places to grab text, image/artwork, and video content. Your teachers are already accessing different resources online to support and complement their teaching. Unfortunately, many teachers teach in a silo with few opportunities to share this type of information. You can support teachers in sharing their favorite resources by dedicating five to ten minutes at the next all-staff meeting to a crowdsourcing activity where they share their favorite online text, image and/or video resources on Padlet Wall or TodaysMeet backchannel.

asynchronous discussion to encourage students to analyze and discuss what conclusions they can draw based on the details of the image.

It's important for teachers to consider what they are asking students to do, either after or while they are viewing the flipped content. Flipping instruction is most effective when teachers make students do something with that information. There are a range of strategies that teachers can use to both flip and engage.

PRODUCING AND PUBLISHING YOUR OWN FLIPPED VIDEOS

If teachers want to create and publish their own video content, it helps to approach the task in three steps: (1) create content, (2) record, and (3) publish.

Step 1: Creating Content

There are two main strategies for creating flipped content. Teachers can record a screencast or a movie. Some teachers prefer to create multimedia presentations using online presentation tools, such as PowerPoint, Keynote, Google Slides, or Prezi; while other teachers who want to demonstrate a process or explain a concept may want to record themselves actually walking through a series of steps, performing an experiment, or writing on a whiteboard as they explain concepts.

Step 2: Recording Videos or Screencasts

Depending on the style of video the teacher wants to create, there are several options for recording that content. Teachers need to use an application that works with the devices they already own.

FIGURE 11.8 Devices and Applications Teachers Can Use to Create Video Content

DEVICE	APPLICATIONS
iPad	Educreations ShowMe
Mac	Quicktime (free program on Macs)
PC	Screencast-O-Matic Camtasia Snagit

Step 3: Exporting to YouTube or a Video Hosting Site

Once teachers have successfully recorded a screencast or movie, they can export their video to an online location where it can be viewed and shared. Alternatively, a video can be uploaded directly from the device where it is saved to YouTube or another video hosting site like SchoolTube.

LINKS TO LEADERSHIP: BUILDING CAPACITY

School leaders can support teachers interested in creating their own content by arranging for professional development focused on helping them create, record, and publish their videos. Designing a flipped classroom training that functions more as a playground experience where teachers work together to create a video decreases anxiety about the process. Are their teacher trailblazers on your campus already flipping their classrooms? If so, can you ask them to lead a fun, hands-on session for teachers interested in experimenting with video creation?

What Are Some of the Challenges Associated With the Flipped Classroom?

There are challenges and benefits to using the Flipped Classroom. Figure 11.9 identifies common challenges and offers creative solutions for addressing those challenges.

FIGURE 11.9 Challenges and Solutions for Using the Flipped Classroom

	CHALLENGES	SOLUTIONS
Lack of Access to Technology Outside of School	Many teachers are concerned about disenfranchising students who don't have access to technology beyond the classroom. Students without easy access can struggle to access instruction in this model.	There are several strategies teachers can employ to ensure that students with limited or no access outside of school can get the information in a flipped model. 1. Teachers can burn videos onto DVDs or save them on flash drives that can be checked out in a similar fashion to a library book. 2. If teachers are flipping with text or images, a print version can be provided to students who need them. 3. Teachers can combine the flipped classroom concept with the Station Rotation Model and plan an in-class flip. (For more on the in-class flip, see p. 161.)

	CHALLENGES	SOLUTIONS
Students Who Do Not Complete Homework	Teachers are uncertain how to handle students who do not complete their homework and come to class without the necessary instruction needed to apply the information.	Teachers must have a plan in place for students who have not done their homework. 1. If teachers have computers, they can allow students who did not see the flipped instruction to watch it while the rest of the class moves on to the creative application activity. 2. Teachers without technology can ask students to silently observe a group at work, applying concepts to learn from what their peers are doing, and take notes on what they observe.
Time It Takes to Create Content	Time is a precious commodity for any educator, and the prospect of investing a lot of time into designing flipped lessons and recording flipped videos is daunting.	Teachers concerned about time investment should check out read-to-use content before spending hours creating their own videos. There are tons of resources where teachers can grab content to experiment with the flipped classroom. If students respond positively to this inverse model, then teachers can decide whether or not they want to create their own videos. It's worth noting that once a teacher has recorded video tutorials, explanations, and/or lectures, they can be used over and over, potentially saving a teacher time in the long run.

In-Class Flip

The in-class flip is a strategy that combines the Flipped Classroom Model with the Station Rotation Model to address many of the concerns teachers have about student access outside of class, and what to do with kids who fail to complete their homework. Instead of sending the flipped instruction home with students to read or watch at home, the flipped content becomes an online learning station in class. Students can still have a degree of control over the pace of their learning in a station. They can pause a video, look up a word, or ask peers for clarification. Then, students can work to apply the flipped information in a subsequent station where they work closely with their peers to problem solve. Just like in the traditional Flipped Classroom Model, the teacher can assist as needed to answer questions, lend support, and act like a tutor helping students as they work.

If teachers want to plan a Station Rotation lesson with an in-class flip, the order and design of the stations is important because students cannot be asked to apply information they haven't seen yet. In the example lesson shown in Figure 11.10, there are five stations; however, the fifth station is intentionally left empty in the first rotation because students have not yet completed the in-class flip station.

The second to last station (#4) in Figure 11.10 is the flipped instruction station. The last station (#5) is the apply station. Students populate the first four stations in the Station Rotation for round one, then they all shift over one station for the second rotation so that Station #1 is empty, and the students who saw the flipped content in Station #4 move to Station #5 where they apply that information, as pictured in Figure 11.11.

This design ensures that students have seen the information they need to effectively work together to apply that information. Combining the Station Rotation Model and the Flipped Classroom with the in-class flip moves all parts of the flipped lesson into the classroom. This approach to the Flipped Classroom is particularly useful for elementary teachers, students without access to technology or internet beyond the classroom, and for students who frequently fail to complete homework assignments prior to class.

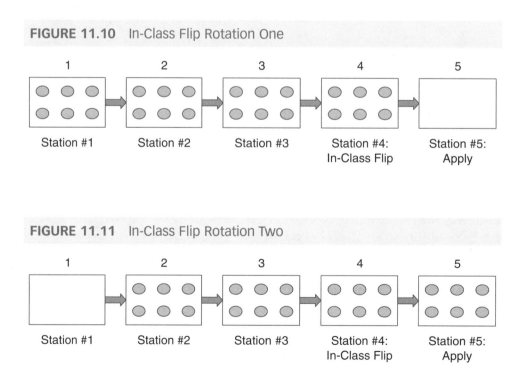

FIGURE 11.10 In-Class Flip Rotation One

| 1 | 2 | 3 | 4 | 5 |

Station #1   Station #2   Station #3   Station #4:   Station #5:
                                          In-Class Flip   Apply

FIGURE 11.11 In-Class Flip Rotation Two

| 1 | 2 | 3 | 4 | 5 |

Station #1   Station #2   Station #3   Station #4:   Station #5:
                                          In-Class Flip   Apply

WRAPPING IT UP

The Flipped Classroom Model shifts the transfer of information online and pulls the practice and application phase of learning into the classroom. The benefit of this inversion is that students can control the pace of their learning at home, and they have the added support of a class full of peers with whom they can work to apply concepts or information. If they are practicing in the classroom, they also have access to the subject area expert. The teacher can circulate, answer questions, offer support, and administer more formative assessments to gauge comprehension.

Although the conversation often focuses on flipping instruction with videos, teachers can access a wealth of online resources to flip with text, images, and video. It's important that teachers explore the resources available to them before investing large amounts of time into creating their own content. If they decide to create their own content, there are several different tools they can use to create, record, and publish their flipped content.

As teachers embrace a blended approach to learning, they need to design flipped lessons that pair the activity with the best learning environment. When transferring information online, it's crucial to flip *and* engage students to maximize the effectiveness of this model. If students are accessing information online, teachers need to think about how they can also use online tools to engage students around that information to improve comprehension and retention.

The in-class flip marries the Station Rotation Model and the Flipped Classroom Model. The in-class flip moves all parts of the flipped classroom into the classroom so that students read or view the flipped content in one station and apply that information in another station. This is especially helpful for elementary teachers or teachers concerned about lack of access outside of the classroom.

BOOK STUDY QUESTIONS

1. What are the biggest benefits and/or challenges to using the Flipped Classroom Model? Are there any challenges or obstacles you are concerned about that were not addressed in this chapter? If so, what are they and how can you overcome these challenges?

2. Do your students have access to technology outside of school? If you are not sure, how can you get this information (e.g., student survey)? If there

are access issues outside of class, could you use the in-class flip in combination with the Station Rotation Model?

3. How much time do you spend each day and/or week presenting information? When you present information, do you use lecture, video, and/or readings? Given the strategies you currently use to transfer information to students, what type of media do you think is the best fit for use in a Flipped Classroom Model?

4. What strategies can you employ to both flip and engage students online to improve comprehension? How can you use the online environment to connect students around the flipped content and drive higher-order thinking? How can you assess students to ensure they were viewing the flipped content?

5. If you spent less time lecturing in class, what can you do with the extra time in class? What types of activities can you design to foster student-centered learning and collaboration to maximize the collective intelligence in your classroom?

6. If you are a teacher, is there any additional support you need in terms of the Links to Leadership section of this chapter? How can teacher trailblazers and school leaders help to support you? How can you make sure you get the support you need?

CHAPTER 12

Other Models and Possibilities

Learning should look like people are interacting with each other, learning from each other's mistakes, a teacher facilitating an activity, but not simply doing the work for the students or giving them answers. Learning how to learn new things from each other and using resources rather than specific answers.

—Laura Malfavon, 10th Grade

INDIVIDUALIZED MODELS AND POSSIBILITIES

Chapters 9 and 10 provided insight into whole group and small group personalization through the group rotation models. These models are often great starting points for more traditional schools to begin their blended learning integrations. This chapter steps beyond the group setting into more individualized blended learning experiences, starting with the Individual Rotation/ Playlist Model and the A La Carte Model. We also explore some possibilities that extend beyond them. To achieve a pinnacle of personalization and connectivity in learning, it is imperative we remain open to these possibilities by approaching the implementation of blended practice with creativity and an iterative mindset.

This chapter

- outlines the Individual Playlist Model and its benefits;
- provides strategies for designing a playlist experience;
- outlines the A La Carte Model and its benefits;
- provides strategies for designing an A La Carte experience; and
- explores connected blended learning experiences beyond existing models.

The Individual Playlist Model involves an advanced level of core tool integration and data management at the individual student level. Student ownership is increased, and teachers focus primarily on facilitation of learning. These qualities place The Individual Playlist Model further along the *Blended Learning Roadmap* in Phase 3: Expansion. The A La Carte Model can be introduced during Phase 1 or Phase 2 with the right support structure in place for students enrolled in online courses.

INDIVIDUAL ROTATIONS AND PLAYLISTS DEFINED

In an Individual Rotation Model, students move through digital and offline learning on a highly personalized path in a face-to-face environment. The Christensen Institute defines the Individual Rotation Model as "a course or subject in which each student has an individualized playlist and does not necessarily rotate to each available station or modality. An algorithm or teacher(s) sets individual student schedules" (Clayton Christensen, 2015, p. 1). Sometimes teachers include students in the creation of the schedule to give them control over some combination of the learning content, order, and/or mode of learning.

At The Summit Schools in California and Washington, during the week students move between personalized learning online, project time, reading time, community time, and mentor meetings using a playlist model. In this setup, students have agency within their Personalized Learning Plans (PLPs), "to set goals, access learning resources, submit work, and track their progress" (Summit Public Schools, 2015, p. 1). Within the personalized learning time, students learn via adaptive software, which drives students forward based on algorithmic assessment of their progress. In mentor meetings, students and teachers plan collaboratively to set goals, monitor progress, and design personal projects. Though Summit Schools use their model across the curriculum, some schools use an individual rotation model for one subject.

MS 88 is a large middle school in Brooklyn that transitioned from a traditional practice to an individual rotation model using the School of One curriculum. After her visit to the school, author Tina Rosenberg shared an in-action observation in the *New York Times* article "Reaching Math Students One by One."

> The classroom is the size of four rooms, its divisions marked with shelving and different colored carpet and chairs. When I visited last month, all four seventh-grade math teachers and some aides circulated, teaching 120 students as a team. As math class begins, students find their names on airport-style monitors outside the room, which tell them where to go. The different areas are named for high schools in Brooklyn. . . . The monitors also tell the students which of several learning modalities they will use. That day, some answered questions at a computer. A few feet away, others did work sheets in pairs. Five students sat at a table with a teacher, solving equations. At one end

of the room, Reisman [a math teacher] worked with 23 students on a multiday probability project. (Rosenberg, 2015, paras. 9, 10, 11)

Figure 12.1 illustrates the characteristics of an Individual Rotation or Playlist Model in comparison with the group rotation models explored in previous chapters.

FIGURE 12.1 Playlist Model Versus Group Rotation Models

GROUP ROTATIONS	BOTH (IN MIDDLE)	INDIVIDUAL ROTATIONS
• highly synchronous • teacher designs groups, rotations, and schedules • small group instruction • teacher at teacher station leads instruction for small groups as they rotate in	• use of digital curriculum and data • some student agency over pace, order, or content • projects used to foster collaboration • students doing different tasks around the room	• highly asynchronous • often algorithm determines rotation order and individual schedules • individual instruction • teacher mobile, checking in with students

LINKS TO LEADERSHIP: MANAGING TECHNOLOGY PLATFORMS

The selection of platforms to use across the curriculum necessitates simplicity and purpose. Teachers and students can grow frustrated trying to remember how to log into various platforms that do not speak to one another. In an Individual Rotation Model, where students are online and in multiple resources for learning, the use of one learning management system or organizational tool to enable quick access to this variety of resources is essential. School leaders and technology integrators can help ensure students spend more time learning by facilitating the thoughtful design of a central resource hub for accessing digital tools and curriculum. Examples of these may include a resources section of a Learning Management Software like Schoology, or a dashboard organization tool like Symbaloo, which allows for teachers to create and share a launch spot for multiple class resources.

What Are the Benefits of the Individual Playlist Model?

The main benefits of using a playlist model over a station rotation model are

1. increased student agency on an individual level;

2. deeper personalization of learning; and

3. students can pace according to readiness.

Designing and Supporting Individual Playlists

When planning an Individual Rotation lesson, you want to keep in mind the learner's preferred mode of learning and use tools like a learning style inventory. There are several examples of inventories, such as the Multiple Intelligences Quiz by Edutopia (www.edutopia.org/multiple-intelligences-assessment). Providing multiple modes for learning is a key feature of this model and ensures differentiation for each student. Some students may pick up a new concept via video lesson, while others can benefit from tinkering first and then watching a video. To lock all learners into a digital playlist that only engages them in watch, read, and practice mode sacrifices the personalization of the learning *process* for that of content and outcome, which can mean that students are consistently demonstrating their learning outcomes in limited forms. Thus, a playlist consisting of multimodal learning experiences is key to maintaining the integrity of the personalized practice.

Figure 12.2 illustrates how a playlist can be constructed to allow for the personalization of content, process, and outcome in addition to some community learning time. In this morning schedule illustration, the larger circles indicate whole class or community building time where the value of the face-to-face environment can be maximized. The smaller circles represent items on a student's playlist which may vary by subject, be moved around in order, and provide choice between modes of learning to ensure multimodal design.

FIGURE 12.2 Multimodal and Community Oriented Playlist Design; PL = "Playlist"

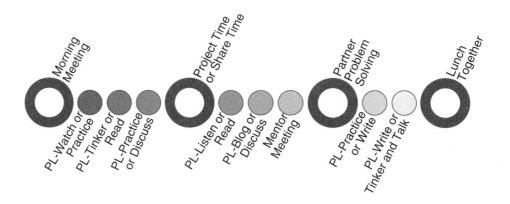

 Whereas Figure 12.2 suggests a daily sequence of learning activities, Figure 12.3 provides a learning space design to complement this sequence. In this type of learning space, students choose their location in the room based on their preferred order of the playlist activities. Student control of sequence, pace, and type of learning makes the Playlist Model especially conducive to fostering student ownership. In addition to cultivating

FIGURE 12.3 Multimodal and Community Oriented Playlist Classroom Design; PL = "Playlist"

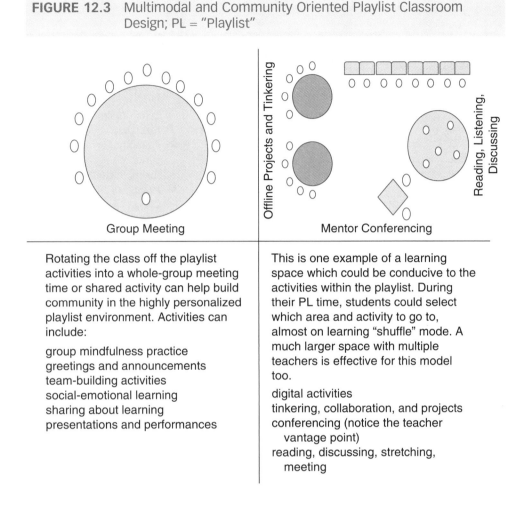

Group Meeting	Mentor Conferencing
Rotating the class off the playlist activities into a whole-group meeting time or shared activity can help build community in the highly personalized playlist environment. Activities can include: group mindfulness practice greetings and announcements team-building activities social-emotional learning sharing about learning presentations and performances	This is one example of a learning space which could be conducive to the activities within the playlist. During their PL time, students could select which area and activity to go to, almost on learning "shuffle" mode. A much larger space with multiple teachers is effective for this model too. digital activities tinkering, collaboration, and projects conferencing (notice the teacher vantage point) reading, discussing, stretching, meeting

agency of learning, this type of learning environment also builds soft skills, such as collaboration, compromise, and respect in sharing a workspace.

Building Community

With so many distinctive pathways in the Individual Rotation Model, students move through a playlist or rotation at a different pace or in a different order and spend less time engaged in the same mode of learning at the same time with their peers. Plus, the content and outcomes of learning can vary greatly from student to student in these models.

Teachers should aim for "rough synchronization" when designing individual rotations. According to a Harvard Business School study of online learning and collaboration, "rough synchronization" is important to peer conversations and collaboration, two critical factors in engaged online learning (Anand, Hammond, & Narayanan, 2015, p. 1, para. 8). Playlists can be set

FIGURE 12.4 Building Community in Asynchronous Environments

FACE-TO-FACE STRATEGIES	DIGITAL SPACE STRATEGIES	CURRICULAR STRATEGIES
• Create time during the day for meeting, sharing, and discussing learning • Advisory programs and mindfulness practices • Extracurricular programs • Class partnerships • Drop-everything-and-share • Learning commons for collaboration	• Class blogging and discussions • Online reading and extracurricular clubs • Team competitions • Class media accounts to build sense of community and sharing	• Project-based learning by shared passions synchronized • Blogging about learning • Combination of some synchronous and some asynchronous learning • Pacing or passion cohorts with shared targets

with modular due dates (or a day's list of lessons to complete), and students can have flexibility in their completion of them. This helps keep students somewhat together in their movement through curricular experiences while still enabling differentiation of order, pace, and content.

Still, there are other ways that teachers can work toward community building and shared learning moments even when students are not learning at the same pace or sharing the same content. At a charter school, Carpe Diem in Yuma, Arizona, students work in a common space, the learning center, which engages students in project collaboration with each other and teachers. Figure 12.4 suggests a list of strategies for strengthening a sense of community and culture within a mostly online experience.

Jan Keating, founding principal of Stanford Online High School, an independent school for gifted students, shared strategies she used to help a fully online program build community and school spirit. Many of these strategies can be applied to a playlist model within a face-to-face environment.

Vignette: Jan Keating, founding principal of Stanford Online High School

Students who attend the Stanford Online High School have opportunities to connect with each other in a number of different ways. They attend class synchronously online each week with the other students in the class. They attend a short homeroom period each week. Homeroom is used to help students get to know each other, as well as to disseminate the weekly school announcements. There are all school assemblies, holiday gatherings, such as the annual Halloween costume party, Club Fair, fall student government speeches and subsequent elections, and forty plus clubs that meet regularly. The student government host various activities throughout the year, including a "Spirit Week," where students are asked to dress according to a variety of themes. All of these activities take place online.

One of the biggest surprises for me when I moved from the traditional school setting to the Stanford Online High School was how well I got to know the students and parents, given the majority of our interactions took place online. Instructors often tell me that they feel they know their students as well or perhaps even better than if they were teaching at a brick-and-mortar School. Students comment to me that they love the fact they have friends all over the world. The simple truth is that when you are in an online classroom interacting with other students and your instructors every day, the "online-ness" of the experience fades into the background, and you become fully engaged in what is going on in the class. As time goes on, interacting online with people becomes much more natural and normal.

What Is the Teacher's Role During an Individual Playlist Experience?

A common misunderstanding of the Individual Playlist Model is that it devalues the role of the teachers and prioritizes the role of digital curriculum. This misconception is not only erroneous but harmful because students left to learn from programs often lose valuable learning time off task and may not understand or retain what they are learning. The role of the teacher is paramount to the success of the Individual Rotation Model. Teachers must identify each student's modality of learning, select the right tools for learning, facilitate engagement, and provide right-type/right-time instruction and feedback along the way. In many ways, teachers facilitating this model of learning have to be even more mobile, engaged, and responsive to student needs than in a more teacher-centered environment. The role of an individual playlist teacher includes, but is not limited to

- mentoring students;
- selecting digital tools and curriculum;
- creating projects and playlists;
- facilitating online discussions and face-to-face shared moments;
- building class culture and community;
- assessing student progress through formative measures;
- providing timely feedback and encouragement to keep students engaged;

- teaching and coaching students along the way;

- collaborating with students in setting personalized goals, strategies, and playlist content/order; and

- walking around and constantly providing feedback, direction, encouragement, and instruction within the environment.

LINKS TO LEADERSHIP: HELPING TEACHERS TO FACILITATE LEARNING

A teacher shifting from a group model to an individual one must be comfortable monitoring multiple learning activities at once and cycling the class into and out of synchronized learning. Planning also becomes more modular with pieces that are synchronized, and others that allow for individual student choice. It's important to provide teachers with training and tools to design a more agile, modular day or week and help teachers design a template for such planning. Additionally, leaders may need to adjust observation and professional growth rubrics to align with indicators more often seen in this type of environment, as more traditional practice indicators can leave teachers feeling misaligned with expectations. Finally, as teachers are highly engaged in tracking individual progress via digital tools in this model, training on how to interpret and respond to learning data is essential for teacher confidence.

Things to consider when planning to shift from a group model to an individual one:

- Allowance for learning modes
- Maintenance of connectedness through asynchronous learning
- Assessment for understanding and feedback loop
- Organization of workflow and lesson delivery

A La Carte Model Defined

The A La Carte Model derives its name from the practice of selecting one item in isolation from the others on the list of offerings. Schools provide a program of courses on site, but sometimes students require or desire a course outside of these program choices. In the A La Carte Model, schools meet these needs by allowing students to select one or more courses from an array of online offerings by a third party. These selections supplement what is on the school's menu of offerings. Many schools provide a time and space during the school day for students to work on these online courses in addition to an on-site facilitator to support students in course completion. A La Carte is considered a blended learning model in a different manner than the other models because the experience is not necessarily a combination of online and face-to-face within the course, but rather a combination of the two modes of blended learning through course offerings that are mainly or fully one or the other.

The A La Carte Model is one of the earliest ways where online learning made its way into K–12 schools as more and more fully online courses became available to students in brick-and-mortar schools. According to a 2011 Innosight Institute's study titled *The Rise of K–12 Blended Learning* conducted from 2000 to 2010, the number of K–12 students enrolled in online courses grew exponentially from just forty-five thousand to over four million (Staker, 2011, p. 7). Schools look to online enrollment to solve a variety of needs, including, but not limited to, the following:

- Scheduling Solutions: In the creation of the master schedule, schools often face scheduling conflicts difficult to resolve with internal solutions. A course or course level may only be available at specific times which may or may not fit a student's other courses. Enrollment in an online course equivalent offers a way to resolve scheduling conflicts that otherwise might force a change in program for a student.

- Credit Recovery: Increasingly, schools seek online learning as a solution to help students recover credits from previously failed or missed courses. Though efficient, it should be noted that this practice draws some criticism as critical student support can vary greatly from class to class.

- Increased Course Offering: School leaders must prioritize core and high demand courses within their school, often sacrificing lower attended courses or more specialized courses where necessary. School leaders look to online learning as a solution to overcome the challenge of staffing and sustaining specialized programs.

- Dual Enrollment: Dual enrollment is a longstanding model for high school students seeking to earn college credit through school partnerships with universities. As online learning grows more prevalent in higher education, the dual enrollment experience is opening to include some online courses.

- Meeting Graduation Requirements: According to The National Conference of State Legislatures (NCSL), five states now include online education as a high school graduation requirement: Arkansas, Virginia, Florida, Michigan, and Alabama (NCSL, 2016, p. 1, para. 9).

Grandview Preparatory School in Boca Raton, Florida, was among the earliest 1:1 laptop and blended learning programs. Head of School Jackie Westerfield explained how A La Carte enrollment became one of the first forms of blended learning to emerge within the school's K–12 setting.

In 1997, Grandview Preparatory School was founded on progressive principles regarding personalization, even though the technological tools available at that time were just emerging. Our founding vision centered on using the tools of the new century to empower student learning in ways previously unimagined. As an early adopter, we did not have the luxury of knowing how fast the technologies would change.

The first available tools included online courses that changed the learning model in two significant ways. First, online courses supplemented our existing brick-and-mortar offerings by enabling students to choose from a wider selection of courses than our school could typically provide. Second, the format of these courses made it possible for students to 'learn on demand' rather than follow the traditional bell schedule and pacing. Even prior to the development of streaming technologies, these two changes alone made it possible to better customize the learning experience at our smaller, independent school.

The implementation challenges of online courses center, as they always do, on the human resources available to supplement the experience. While self-pacing and flexibility are benefits, students still need face time with teachers to mentor and guide them through difficulties. Our greatest implementation successes have been built on providing strong real-time facilitation for students, either physically on our campus, at a Starbucks, or even via video chat applications.

How Do Schools Select Course Providers for A La Carte Integration?

Just as there are numerous digital curriculum providers for schools to select from in designing rotation models, there are several online course providers and fully online schools that allow for A La Carte enrollment. These range from public to fee-based and vary state to state depending on the structure of the program. For example, Florida Virtual School (FLVS) was the first online public school offering free public enrollment to all state residents. From its start in 1997, FLVS has grown to include both a state program and a global tuition-based program available for students to earn credits for individual courses, and a diploma after completion of all graduation requirements. For its public program, Florida students in both public and independent schools can enroll in courses free of charge. Schools in the state have engaged FLVS as a partner in curricular offering expansion. Recognizing the demand for its program beyond state lines, Florida Virtual School opened its FLVS Global Program in 2000. On average, FLVS teaches 150,000 students annually and has dedicated teams to provide school implementation support to onsite facilitators. As the program has evolved, FLVS has worked to incorporate teacher visits to school sites for a more blended experience.

Sr. Director of Business Development & Solutions for FLVS, Dr. Polly Haldeman, explained,

> Most of our courses offer live lessons. In addition, for the Blended Learning Communities, we try really hard and start planning early, to pair schools with teachers who are near them geographically, and if not, then we at least make a concerted effort to have teacher pairings that are successful in helping one get to a site. A combination of a Face-to-Face visit, which you can imagine makes those students realize this teacher is real and they care, and the live lessons which do that as well, help engage students. (Haldeman, personal communication, January 26, 2016)

Since FLVS's opening, forty-four states have opened online public virtual schools.

Aside from state supported schools, there are a number of credit rendering national and international course providers, such as K–12, International Academy, and The Keystone School. In selecting the right course provider, schools should think through the following questions to determine if a provider meets the requirements unique to each school and/or district:

- By what standards is the curriculum designed?

- What are the qualifications of the teachers and the screening process?

- What is the learning experience like? Is it mainly traditional, but online to watch/listen/assess, or more interactive, collaborative, and project-based?

- How do students interact with teachers and their peers? What is the protocol for these interactions?

- How accessible are teachers to students, parents, and onsite facilitators? How accessible is tech support?

- Is learning entirely asynchronous or do students participate in scheduled live sessions?

- What are the rules for dropping courses?

- What makes the provider experiences unique compared to other online courses?

At Grandview Preparatory School, teacher and Director of Program Innovation Sam Berey has integrated open source courses and massive open online courses, or MOOCs, into the curriculum through organizations such as EdX and Coursera. Regarding selecting the right courses, Sam emphasizes the importance of engaging content and human interaction:

The most successful classes were those with dynamic instructors (where students could not only tolerate the self-paced videos, but looked forward to them). Overall, finding the right balance in a blended learning course proved to be quite the challenge. My students often yearned for more human interaction, especially since they were used to that in a traditional learning environment. Knowing what I know now, I would spend a significant amount of time screening the blended content before promoting the course. (Sam Berey, interview, March, 2016)

LINKS TO LEADERSHIP: LOGISTICS OF A LA CARTE LEARNING

As leaders work to create successful A La Carte learning models, there are several logistical considerations, including physical space, scheduling, and student monitoring requirements. Questions to consider include:

1. Are students required to be in a specific physical space during the day to complete their course work, and if so, how often?

2. Does the school provide the equipment needed for course connectivity and participation (e.g., some language courses require special headsets)?

3. Are there dedicated spaces for online coursework, and what do the responsibilities of the teacher in this space include?

4. Who is responsible for setting up any required platforms and providing technical support along the way?

What Are the Benefits of the A La Carte Model?

Schools have implemented A La Carte practice to meet a variety of needs; however, the model offers many more benefits to students. Students who have a passion for a particular subject or an accelerated path can delve into more specialized learning through online enrollment. Online learning also offers a chance for K–12 students to build important skills in preparation for online enrollment in college, and in preparation for career success. This college and career readiness goal is critical for students in today's digital era where collaboration with team members one never meets in person is now more the norm than the exception. Students who take an online course have the opportunity to broaden their peer group and practice this type of digital collaboration with peers and their teachers.

The main benefits of using an A La Carte Model are

- supplementing the face-to-face settings of curricular programs to offer more learning options to students

- personalizing course offerings to meet student interests and readiness
- receiving learning anytime/anywhere for a full course experience
- building a supported bridge to success in online learning before college
- involving a broader peer group for connected learning

Designing and Supporting A La Carte

Despite the bulk of the learning experience conducted online through third parties, schools play an important role in designing a successful path for their students. One way schools can effectively meet the responsibilities of this role is by appointing an onsite facilitator for online learning. This individual can be any number of people within the school, including a teacher, advisor, academic leader, or guidance counselor. Schools need to determine whether to centralize or decentralize this role by appointing either one individual to manage and support all online enrollment, or by assigning different facilitators to each student. Depending on the workload and resources available, schools often appoint facilitator responsibilities in addition to teaching or counseling responsibilities.

Facilitators provide vital support for students leading up to and then during online learning experiences. Dr. Polly Haldeman of Florida Virtual School indicated this onsite blended learning specialist role is often a "make it or break it" component of the student experience in an A La Carte Model. Haldeman said,

> That connection has been the strongest thing that has been the most directly impactful to students. The kinds of things that they do, which used to be roadblocks in the past, is work with scheduling, lab time, lab setup, where the phone is in the room, logistical stuff that we used to take for granted would be in place, now make things like facilitating strong online lessons and synchronized online discussions. (Polly Haldeman, personal communication, January 26, 2016)

As the teachers on the face-to-face side of this blended learning experience, facilitators can leverage their rapport with and knowledge of the student to guide the learning experience. For example, if a student's learning style is less visual and more tactile or social, an online experience that is more transactional (teacher provides the work and student turns it in) may be a mismatch for the student. In this scenario, the facilitator's understanding of the student's learning style and other factors can inform a better fit for course selection, or determine ways in which the learning can become more interactive through collaboration with the online teacher. Facilitators can aid students in communicating effectively with their online teachers when they need clarification or instructional support and can provide onsite guidance during course completion. The proximity of the facilitator to the student on a regular basis allows for ongoing intervention and support when challenges arise.

The facilitator can also help onboard the student into the course platform and ensure that he or she feels comfortable in the new learning environment. Methods for such onboarding of students is covered in greater detail in Chapter 8; however, the basic outline includes tech training, expectation clarification, and ongoing support. It is very important to take into account and plan for the high levels of support often required for students to successfully complete an online course.

Schools can provide additional support for students by allocating space and time for students to work on their online courses. Wherever it is possible to build the time into the student's schedule, it is advantageous to do so. However this may not be possible if students are taking a course in addition to a full load. Setting up time for students to meet briefly with their onsite facilitators on a frequent basis is an alternative way to dedicate time and attention to the online course during the school day. In addition to the issue of time, schools can help students by designating spaces conducive to online learning, preferably in proximity to the onsite facilitator. Often schools use learning commons, libraries, or labs to meet this student support need. Where the onsite facilitator is not proximal to the space, it is helpful to provide some training to teachers who manage the space so that they can partner in the support of online learning within the school.

Things to consider when planning for A La Carte implementation:

- course providers and quality assessment
- learning styles and readiness of individual learners
- physical space and time for learning
- structures of ongoing student support in the face-to-face environment
- communication protocols
- responsibilities for facilitator, student, online teacher, and parents

LINKS TO LEADERSHIP: ROLE DEFINITION AND POLICY

Because A La Carte practice brings in entire courses from external providers, there are important factors to take into account internally, and in building the partnership between course providers and the school. School leaders need to establish a protocol for reviewing course offerings for curricular and pedagogical fit; define the roles of each constituent onsite and online; create structures of student onboarding and support; and determine how grades and credits are reflected on school records. The use of an online learning contract between the school, student, and parents is a helpful tool to ensure that everyone is fully aware of the policies and responsibilities of each constituent group.

Building Capacity Through Onsite Facilitator Training and Networking

Facilitating A La Carte learning is a different experience than teaching a class and requires specific training. Course providers often offer teacher facilitator onboarding so that teachers feel comfortable with the platform used by the student. Facilitators also benefit from sharing resources and networking with other facilitators. For example, as part of their teacher support services, FLVS provides an online portal for facilitators to share resources. Dr. Haldeman referred to this space as a "community of learners" where teachers mentor each other and share tools. School leaders should encourage this type of connection for onsite facilitators.

Beyond the Models

Students are already figuring out how to take learning into their own hands. Speakers and authors Scott Young and Jay Cross have built expansive knowledge, credibility, and careers through self-study and test taking via a patchwork of online experiences (Young, 2012). However, even younger students have gone outside of school walls or entirely abandoned traditional learning to follow a more personalized and passion-based learning path. One such student, Timothy Doner, taught himself twenty languages during his teen years by listening to music, frequenting cafes or other target language spots in New York, and Skyping with a global network he built along the way. Another teenager, Logan LaPlante, calls his approach to personalizing his education "hackschooling." In his TED Talk, Logan shares,

> I don't use any one particular curriculum and I'm not dedicated to any one particular approach. I hack my education. I take advantage of opportunities in my community and through a network of my friends and family. It's like a remix or a mashup of learning; it's flexible, opportunistic. (LaPlante, TED-talk, YouTube video)

These network opportunities include connecting with teachers and mentors, like the "great speakers around the nation" who Logan says he received feedback from in order to develop his voice as a writer. Logan goes on to say that hackschooling can be used anywhere by anyone, "even traditional schools (LaPlante, TED-talk, YouTube video)."

The following is a list of "What if" questions that school leaders can consider when thinking creatively about new models and possibilities.

- What if students could design their own schedules for most of the day?
- What if schools could open their already existing courses to online enrollment to students in other schools through course sharing?
- What if students interacted with experts to guide them through projects, instead of requiring teachers to lead all learning?

WRAPPING IT UP

This chapter covers one of the earliest blended learning models (A La Carte), and one of the most recent models to emerge (Individual Rotation). These models are alike in that a sizeable portion of student learning takes place online. However, the Individual Playlist Model presents more face-to-face interaction within a traditional school as opposed to the A La Carte Model where the interaction between the learner and teacher is online. In implementing a playlist experience for students, schools provide a bridge to developing greater agency and skill in learning online. The learning experiences in an Individual Playlist Model help to build the competencies needed for successful completion of a course in an A La Carte fashion or via online enrollment in higher education.

As blended learning has grown to scale, the early models in the implementation of classroom technology served to provide necessary structure and confidence in changing schools. However, opportunities to leverage technology for learning and human connectivity are endless. To actualize new opportunities, teachers and leaders need to employ creativity in solving new problems, and in doing so, can take us beyond the models currently in place.

BOOK STUDY QUESTIONS

1. What are the biggest benefits and/or challenges to using the Individual Playlist or the A La Carte Model? Are there any challenges or obstacles you are concerned with that are not addressed in this chapter? If so, what are they and how can you overcome these challenges?

2. What would a playlist lesson look like in your class? In what ways could you work to keep it multimodal?

3. How does the classroom environment, and the teacher's role in managing it, change in an Individual Playlist Model? What strategies can you use to keep "withitness" (a term to describe a teacher's awareness of what is going on in all parts of the classroom at all times) intact while students work at their own pace on different tasks?

4. If you are a teacher, is there any additional support you need in terms of the Links to Leadership section of this chapter? How can teacher trailblazers and leaders in leadership positions help to support you? How can you make sure you get the support you need?

5. What would "rough synchronization" look like in your class/subject? What other strategies can you think of to build community in an asynchronous environment?

6. Have you had experience coaching a student through an online class before? What techniques did you use to facilitate successful completion of the class?

7. What other "What If?" questions can you brainstorm to extend connected learning possibilities?

PART 4

Blended Learning: The Roadmap to Personalization

INTRODUCTION

In our work with schools, we are often asked by school leaders: *How can you tell if it is working? In what ways can we see evidence of effective practice in the classroom?* In this final part, as you proceed through Phase 2 and Phase 3 of the *Blended Learning Roadmap,* we share resources for assessing the effectiveness and impact of the program in a visible way. We discuss the milestones of each phase, take a "Dive into the Classroom" to see how it looks in action, and encourage you to be on the lookout for some common pitfalls.

The answer to these questions, however, goes beyond the scope of what can be seen and measured in a walk-through. Instead, it can be *felt* around the community. The real indicator of progress is the buzz of innovation evident in teachers trying new techniques, learning from each other, sharing valuable resources, and stretching beyond their understanding of the models. This extends to students trying new tools, learning from each other, sharing their creative endeavors, and stretching themselves beyond their own expectations. Personalization is not measured in data; it is *experienced* in how closely we understand our students as people. It cannot be achieved through technology alone.

> Personalization is not measured in data; it is experienced in how closely we understand our students as people.

In your journey through this book, you can see that we discussed technology and tools at length. However, the best use of technology in learning is to bring teachers and students closer together. As you continue through these next steps, do so with this long game in mind, considering not just how to observe and adjust through iterative practice, but also how to generate the buzz of innovation that continues to bring you closer to the target of personalization.

CHAPTER 13

The Roadmap
to Personalization

Who Is They?

Dean I. Zweiman, 5th Grade

Who is they?

We see the future as robotics and new technology.

We say that "they" will invent these things.

But, who is they?

Will these robots and futuristic possibilities emerge?

Without a they to create them?

Will there be a they?

Can the future exist as we see it?

If there isn't someone to start it?

You are they.

Right now we are preparing students for the unknown. We don't know what world they will face in twenty or even ten years. The single greatest gift we can give them, more than any historical fact, scientific formula, or grammar convention is to help them learn how to learn. When we get really good at this, we help them learn how to learn with *purpose*—defined as learning that is both meaningful to students individually, and valuable to the world. We can then structure their personalized path around that objective. That is the possibility and power of blended learning–a teacher looking at a room of twenty, twenty-five, or even thirty or more students and facilitating a learning experience that honors each one of those learner's unique needs, abilities, and passions. While we may not know what the future looks like, we can paint a clear picture of what type of learning can facilitate preparation for what's to come. Let's take time here to envision the path forward and explore how blended learning looks in action along the rest of the *Roadmap*.

THE PATH FORWARD TO PERSONALIZATION

To illustrate such a path, we need to go back to the *Blended Learning Roadmap*. In Chapter 2, Getting Started, we looked in detail at **Phase 1: Foundations**. Now we look more closely at **Phase 2: Transitions** and **Phase 3: Expansion**. Remember that we acknowledge and recommend a very incremental path toward systemwide transformation. In most cases, the shift to blended learning may require anywhere from three to five years, or sometimes more, depending on the characteristics of a given school or district and their unique challenges with regard to infrastructure, technology, staff proficiency, or other distinctive characteristics. As discussed before, this is okay. More important than transforming your school overnight is setting off in the right direction with your key players sharing the vision and working together.

Phase 2: Transitions

Transitioning means you are somewhere in between point *A* and point *B*. The in-between state can be a confusing place to be since the destination outcomes are not yet met, and it is difficult to understand what metrics to monitor while you are in progress. In Phase 1: Foundations, your leadership efforts focused on stakeholder engagement, assessment, planning, and igniting the creativity of trailblazers through the pre-pilot. In the transition phase, your efforts focused much more on the cycle of conducting a larger pilot, collecting the learnings, iterating, and then expanding on what works. So, what does this look like as you walk the halls of your school, and what are the important metrics to keep in mind?

Dive Into the Classroom

You should begin to see tangible instructional shifts in classrooms as more teachers experiment with new blended models and strategies. It's important for leaders to recognize that most teachers are departing from their comfort zone of teacher-centered instruction, so shifts will be incremental. The ideal pacing varies somewhat from teacher to teacher and even from school to school. As illustrated in Figure 13.1, the elements you should see in classrooms are shifts in the classroom structure and design, greater variety in instructional time between whole group and teacher-led instruction to more frequent student-led, collaborative, and independent work. Through better integration of technology, your teachers should be in position to receive data more frequently and use that data to continually adjust their instruction. As the shift occurs in instruction, you should notice students becoming more

FIGURE 13.1 Phase 2: Evidence of Practice

Courtesy of Redbird Advanced Learning.

active in the learning process while the learning modalities expand to include more opportunities for analysis and application.

As you navigate through the transition phase, pay attention to specific metrics from pilots that inform iteration and then expansion. Table 13.1 outlines the assessment metrics, key considerations, and indicators of readiness for pilot expansion illustrated in Figure 13.1.

TABLE 13.1 Roadmap Metrics

METRIC	KEY CONSIDERATIONS	EXPANSION INDICATORS
Timing and Pacing	• What is the goal of the program, and is the available timing realistic? • When is the ideal time to begin the proper support and assessment window? • How long should the pilot last?	Timing and pacing work to provide support and achieve goals.
Budget	• What are the projected costs? • Are there hidden costs that surface? • Is the funding of expansion sustainable?	Budget is aligned with timing and pacing and is sustainable, including hidden costs.
Student Feedback	• Is the tool/model/program engaging? • Is it easy to use? • Are students having a positive experience? • Is there an impact on learning from a qualitative point of view?	Students respond positively as measured by engagement, disposition toward use, and perceived impact on learning.
Teacher Feedback	• Is the tool/model/program engaging? • Is it easy to use? • Are teachers having a positive experience? • Is there an impact on teaching and learning from a qualitative point of view?	Teachers respond positively as measured by engagement, disposition toward use, and perceived impact on teaching and learning.

(Continued)

TABLE 13.1 (Continued)

METRIC	KEY CONSIDERATIONS	EXPANSION INDICATORS
Learning Outcomes	• How do you expect the tool/ model/program to impact student achievement? • What learning outcomes will you measure and by what assessments? • Over what time period will you seek to measure the impact? • Does the tool/model/program help meet these needs?	Initial indicators show some positive, if not statistically comprehensive correlation. Remember, it can take a few years to gain solid data on student achievement.

Phase 3: Expansion

As you move into **Phase 3: Expansion,** your blended learning implementation is well under way. You are now in position for a full rollout and should see even more visible evidence of practice at scale.

Dive Into the Classroom

As illustrated in Figure 13.2, you should now see deep practice of blended learning, particularly in those classrooms involved throughout the process. Remember that classrooms are now in different phases, but they should all reflect one or a variety of blended learning models covered in Chapters 9 through 12. By this phase, the more advanced teachers are in full facilitator mode, allowing students to engage even more deeply in driving their learning process. These classrooms now allow for significant opportunities for personalization, and are ideally positioned for students to have a role in determining the path of their learning. Teachers are contributing to and reading the data narrative multiple times per week, providing feedback through formative assessment to students, and adjusting instruction on a personalized basis. As we learned, many adaptive digital assessment tools and curriculum tools can make this feedback loop immediate and the instructional pathway adaptive to progress. Routines in the classroom, such as timers for movement and cues for device usage, should be recognizable from class to class. Phase 3 should be marked by active student ownership and student voice, directed to an authentic audience.

As you continue through Phase 3 of the *Blended Learning Roadmap,* keep in mind the continual commitment to the practices started in Phase 2. As the pilots you monitored in the transition phase are expanded or sunsetted, you continue to assess, iterate, and build sustainable practice. The main shift in this phase is one of scaling to full implementation, what had previously been a smaller and more targeted practice. By this phase, the key is in the coordination of tangible items (resources, tools) and intangible factors (attitudes, capacity, motivation) as they expand outward from the pilot phase. In the mainstreaming of the blended process, teachers across the technology

FIGURE 13.2   Evidence of Practice: Phase 3

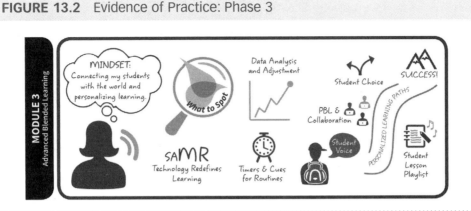

Courtesy of Redbird Advanced Learning.

adoption cycle are brought fully into the fold, which increases the challenges in overall adoption and quality of the implementation. This also is an opportunity for more advanced teachers to serve as champions and coaches for teachers earlier in the process. Tips for scaling pilot components to overcome scaling challenges are outlined in Table 13.2.

ACHIEVING SUSTAINABILITY

Sustainability is one of the most elusive characteristics in K–12 school initiatives. The challenge with so many initiatives is that they start with a bang and end with a whimper (if they ever even get off the ground). The hurdles to creating sustainability are multifold: Many times the proper foundation is not laid for a new initiative and the implementation is shoddy; or the buy-in required from stakeholders is not garnered; or a key leader like the superintendent leaves the district and the grand vision leaves as well. To implement a successful blended learning initiative, sustainability is key. As you envision Phase 3, keep in mind that the key to long-term sustainability rests primarily in the set-up. Essentially, this means that the foundation laid in Phase 1 is most vital. The vision must be set, key stakeholders engaged, honest assessment conducted, and a realistic yet ambitious plan established. If this is the starting point for a blended initiative, then the inevitable hurdles are surmountable.

Though the *Blended Learning Roadmap* is set up in a linear fashion, hopefully, you see a significant degree of cyclicity in it as well, especially around the assessment and iteration phases. This is intentional. Even after a district reaches scale in Phase 3 and is into the Sustain mode, a continued practice of assessment and iteration needs to exist. This helps ensure that best practices continue to emerge and evolve alongside new developments in technology and blended learning pedagogy.

TABLE 13.2 Overcoming Scaling Challenges

COMPONENTS	CONSIDERATIONS	KEY STAKEHOLDERS AND RESOURCES
Device	Was the device usage manageable? What issues did the pilot encounter that could be fixed with iterative planning? For what grades is the same device the best fit, and should other choices be considered? How will device management work at each grade level and at scale?	• IT, Edtech administrator/integrator • Device management software, storage, charging equipment • Policies and procedures for device care
Digital Tool	How did teachers and learners interact with the tool for maximum outcome? What issues did the pilot encounter that could be fixed with iterative planning? For what grades/subjects is the tool a good fit, and are there ways to scaffold use (e.g., enabling different email features for different grades)?	• Tech integrator • Curriculum specialists • Pilot program teachers
Culture	If the pilot group had a positive energy, how can you leverage word of mouth from students and teachers? If the experience was mixed, how can you adjust so as to make the larger experience even better?	• Pilot program teachers and teacher trailblazers • Pilot program students • Team leaders, department leaders
Teacher Capacity	How will all teachers learn how to implement the tool/program? What teacher support needs to be in place? How can you leverage the skill set of the pilot team via proximity to others?	• Pilot program teachers and teacher trailblazers • Engaging, ongoing professional development

THE RESPONSIBILITY OF TEACHING "THEY"

At the opening of this chapter, our 5th-grade poet, Dean, reminds us we are teaching students who are the "they" who will build our future. This is the real reason we need to get this right. Our "modern" school system was created in response to the Industrial Revolution. Factories needed skilled workers with basic literacy, who could focus on a single task that was repeated for hours each day. In response to this demand, education became an assembly line: linear, mechanistic, and standardized. This model worked when the goal was compliance. Innovation is not born of compliance; a new model is needed to unlock the creativity of "they" who are in our classrooms.

As our economy shifted from industry to information, the needs of the workforce also shifted. A new set of skills are required to succeed in our rapidly evolving economy. The workforce needs people to be able to communicate, collaborate, think critically, create, and adapt. These are fundamentally different outputs than what schools were historically producing.

In the most watched Ted Talk of all time, "Do Schools Kill Creativity?," Sir Ken Robinson made the case that schools do, in fact, squash the curiosity and creativity innate in children. Robinson quotes Picasso saying that "all children are born artists. The problem is to remain an artist as we grow up" (Robinson, 2006, Ted Talk). So what happens? Why does the creativity so inherent in children disappear? Robinson asserts that in part it is because schools cultivate a fear of failure. Students are not given the space or freedom to fail, and as a result they lose that magical creativity that characterizes childhood. When this observation is considered using the factory model prototype for schools, this makes sense. A mistake could be costly, or even deadly. By contrast, today our economy depends heavily on creativity and innovation. Sadly, our schools have not adjusted to the needs of an evolving economy; instead, we continue to churn out students who are ill equipped to succeed in life beyond the classroom. Blended learning provides a much needed escape from this failing paradigm.

Even when we examine the innovative example of a student like Logan LaPlante, the "hack schooler" referenced in Chapters 1 and 12, we are still not providing viable alternatives for the majority of students. Logan's model incorporates significant support structures, such as experiential classes, camps, technology and online resources, even social and emotional development. The majority of students rely on schools for these types of essential support structures to help them develop and learn. Though information is more readily available to students today through technology, access to information is fundamentally different than learning. The majority of students absolutely need schools. They need schools to provide structure, support, coaching and positive role models. They need schools to create a healthy environment and facilitate learning. However, they no longer need schools that prioritize the transfer of information. Students have limitless amounts of information at their fingertips. They need schools and teachers to guide them to learn: to find credible information, to make sense of that information, and to apply it in creative ways.

This new role of the school delivers the hallmarks of blended learning as we first presented in Chapter 1:

- **Personalization:** providing unique learning pathways for individual students

- **Connection:** giving learners opportunities to experience learning in collaboration with peers and experts locally and globally

- **Student Agency:** giving learners opportunities to participate in key decisions in their learning experience

- **Creativity:** providing students individual and collaborative opportunities to make things that matter, and to build skills for their future

- **Authentic Audience:** giving students the opportunity to create for a real audience, both locally and globally

Personalized learning should not be solely for the privileged or the lucky. Until very recently, creating this type of learning experience was nearly impossible outside of the privileged or lucky sector of independent schools—for example, specialized school models like Montessori, Waldorf, or alternative special magnet programs. Though none of the hallmarks explicitly reference technology, it is the advent of modern technology that now makes this type of learning experience possible in every classroom and for every child. However, it is possible only to the extent that a teacher is capable of leveraging these new capabilities to engage, empower, and excite learners.

WRAPPING IT UP

In just a few years, all the buzz about "blended" learning will fade, and it will simply be *learning*. Some schools will recognize this transition and get moving in a thoughtful way now. We hope most. Though it may seem a daunting task, the transition toward a successfully scaled blended implementation is both manageable and necessary. When viewed incrementally, taken with ambition and patience, and understood as a collective process requiring the engagement of all stakeholders, the rewards of student learning, engagement, and empowerment will be manifold.

In this book we illustrated this path for district, school leaders, and teachers alike. All of us educators owe Dean, the 5th grader who wrote the poem at the beginning of this chapter, and students just like him all over the world, the effort to meet them where *they* are. The path to that destination is now yours. Good luck!

BOOK STUDY QUESTIONS

1. Where along the *Blended Learning Roadmap* does your school or district exist? How did you get here?

2. Are there any key steps in the process that were missed that should be revisited?

3. Based on your current position, what are the key next steps in your implementation process?

4. What are some of the pitfalls that you experienced or that you anticipate experiencing? How can you address them now or preemptively?

5. How can you use technology to engage, empower, and excite new creativity and reach and teach "they" who are in your classes? How far do you need to travel? Where can you begin, and what is your first destination along the roadmap? Who are your travel companions, and how can you engage and inspire them to join you?

References

7 best practices for getting faculty buy-in for a new LMS. (2016). Schoology.com, author. Retrieved from https://info.schoology.com/rs/601-CPX-764/images/Getting-Faculty-Buy-In-LMS.pdf

Adams, S. (2014). The 10 skills employers most want in 2015 graduates. *Forbes.* Retrieved at www.forbes.com/sites/susanadams/2014/11/12/the-10-skills-employers-most-want-in-2015-graduates/#3f3602ff19f6

Anand, B., Hammond, J., & Narayanan, V. (2015, April 14). *What Harvard Business School has learned about online collaboration from HBX.* Retrieved from https://hbr.org/2015/04/what-harvard-business-school-has-learned-about-online-collaboration-from-hbx

Anderson, M. (2015). How having smartphones (or not) shapes the way teens communicate. *Pew Research Center.* Retrieved from www.pewresearch.org/fact-tank/2015/08/20/how-having-smartphones-or-not-shapes-the-way-teens-communicate

Arney, L. (2015). *Go blended! A handbook for blended technology in schools.* San Francisco, CA: Jossey-Bass.

Aulet, B. (2014). Culture eats strategy for breakfast. *TechCrunch.* Retrieved from http://techcrunch.com/2014/04/12/culture-eats-strategy-for-breakfast/

Ball, A. F. (2015), *Effective professional development for 21st century learning* [Research Paper]. Stanford, CA: Stanford University Graduate School of Education.

Ball, A. F., & Sedlacek, Q. (2015). *Toward an institutional model of teacher professional development* [Research Paper]. Stanford, CA: Stanford University Graduate School of Education.

Barnes, M., & Gonzalez, J. (2015). *Hacking education: 10 quick fixes for every school.* Cleveland, OH: Times 10.

Boston Consulting Group (BCG). (2014). Teachers know best. *Bill & Melinda Gates Foundation.* Retrieved from http://k12education.gatesfoundation.org/wp-content/uploads/2015/04/Gates-PDMarketResearch-Dec5.pdf/

Bray, B., & McClaskey, K. (2013). A step by step guide to personalize learning. *International Society for Technology in Education, 40*(7), 12–19.

Bray, B., & McClasky, K. (2014, June 25). *Personalize learning: Updated personalization vs. differentiation vs. individualization chart version 3.* Retrieved from http://www.personalizelearning.com/2013/03/new-personalization-vs-differentiation.html

Chrome. (n.d.). "What are extensions?" Chrome website, Author. Retrieved from https://developer.chrome.com/extensions

Clayton Christensen Institute. (2015). *Blended learning definitions*. Retrieved from http://www.christenseninstitute.org/blended-learning-definitions-and-models

Clinton, J. M., & Hattie, J. A. C. (2014). Teachers as evaluators: An empowerment evaluation approach. In D. M. Fetterman, S. J. Kaftarian & A. Wandersman (Eds.), *Empowerment evaluation: Knowledge and tools for self-assessment, evaluation capacity building, and accountability*. Thousand Oaks, CA: SAGE.

Couros, G. (2015). *The innovator's mindset* (Kindle). San Diego, CA: Dave Burgess Consulting.

Crowdsourcing. (2006). The white paper version definition. *Crowdsourcing*. Retrieved from http://www.crowdsourcing.com/cs/crowdsourced_softare/

Davis, V. (2015). A guidebook for social media in the classroom. *Edutopia*. Retrieved from http://www.edutopia.org/blog/guidebook-social-media-in-classroom-vicki-davis/

Duncan, A. (2014). Future ready: Building technology infrastructure for learning. *Office of Educational Technology*. Retrieved from https://tech.ed.gov/wp-content/uploads/2014/11/Future-Ready-Schools-Building-Technology-Infrastructure-for-Learning-.pdf

Edsurge. (2016). *Adaptive learning definition*. Retrieved from https://www.edsurge.com/research/special-reports/adaptive-learning/definition

Fullan, M., & Quinn, J. (2016). *Coherence: The right drivers in action for schools, districts, and systems*. Thousand Oaks, CA: Corwin.

Gladwell, M. (2006). *The tipping point: How little things can make a big difference*. New York, NY: Little, Brown and Company.

Guymon, D. (2014, May 29). 6 mistakes you might be making with technology integration. *Getting Smart*. Retrieved from http://gettingsmart.com/2014/05/5-mistakes-might-making-technology-integration/

Harris Poll. (2015). Many more college students still prefer laptops over tablets. *edSurge*. Retrieved from www.edsurge.com/news/2015–09–24-harris-poll-many-more-college-students-still-prefer-laptops-over-tablets

Hattie, J. (2015). *What works best in education: The politics of collaborative expertise*. London, UK: Pearson. Retrieved from https://www.pearson.com/content/dam/corporate/global/pearson-dot-com/files/hattie/150526_ExpertiseWEB_V1.pdf/

Heath, C., & Heath, D. (2010). *Switch: How to change things when change is hard*. New York, NY: Broadway Books.

Horn, M., & Staker, H. (2011, January). *Christensen institute*. Retrieved from http://www.christenseninstitute.org/?publications=the-rise-of-k-12-blended-learning

Horn, M. B., & Staker, H. (2014). *Blended: Using disruptive innovation to improve schools*. San Francisco. CA: Jossey-Bass.

ISTE–International Society for Technology in Education. (2007). *ISTE Standards for Students*. Retrieved from http://www.iste.org/standards/iste-standards/standards-for-students

ISTE–International Society for Technology in Education. (2016). *ISTE Standards for Students*. Retrieved from http://www.iste.org/standards/iste-standards/standards-for-students

LaPlante, L. (2013, February 12). *Hackschooling makes me happy* (YouTube video). *TEDˣ* at University of Nevada. Retrieved from https://www.youtube.com/watch?v=h11u3vtcpaY

Lenhart, A. (2015). Mobile access shifts social media use and other online activities. *Pew Research Center*. Retrieved from www.pewinternet.org/2015/04/09/mobile-access-shifts-social-media-use-and-other-online-activities

McLaughlin, J. (2016). What is organizational culture: Definitions and characteristics? [Video]. *Study.com*. Retrieved from http://study.com/academy/lesson/what-is-organizational-culture-definition-characteristics.html/

McTighe, J., & Wiggins, G. (2012, March). *Understanding by Design® framework*. Alexandria, VA: Association for Supervision and Curriculum Development (ASCD). Retrieved from http://www.ascd.org/ASCD/pdf/siteASCD/publications/UbD_WhitePaper0312.pdf

Morgan, B. (2015). Bring your own device programs on the rise in K–12 school districts. *Crescerance*. Retrieved from http://crescerance.com/blog/2015/06/22/bring-your-own-device-programs-on-the-rise-in-k12-school-districts

National Conference of State Legislatures (NCSL). (2016, April 26). *Online Learning*. Retrieved from http://www.ncsl.org/research/education/online-learning-as-graduation-requirement.aspx

Opitz, B., Ferdinand, N. K., & Mecklinger, A. (2011). Timing matters: The impact of immediate and delayed feedback on artificial language learning. *Frontiers in Human Neuroscience, 5,* 8. Retrieved from http://doi.org/10.3389/fnhum.2011.00008

Parr, S. (2012). Culture eats strategy for lunch. *Fast Company*. Retrieved from http://www.fastcompany.com/1810674/culture-eats-strategy-lunch/

Pink, D. (2009, July). *The puzzle of motivation* [TED Talk]. Retrieved from http://www.ted.com/talks/dan_pink_on_motivation?language=en#t-908119

Richardson, W. (2012, September). *Why school? Why education must change when learning and information are everywhere*. New York, NY: Ted Books and Ted Conferences.

Robinson, K. (2006, Feb.). Do schools kill creativity? [TED Talk]. Retrieved from https://www.ted.com/talks/ken_robinson_says_schools_kill_creativity?language=en

Robinson, V., Lloyd, C., & Rowe, K. (2008). The impact of leadership on student outcomes. *Education Administration Quarterly, 44,* 635–674.

Rosenberg, T. (2015, March 13). Reaching math students one by one. *New York Times*. Retrieved from http://opinionator.blogs.nytimes.com/2015/03/13/reaching-math-students-one-by-one/?_r=1

Rouse, M. (2016). Definition of a learning management system. *Techtarget.com*. Retrieved from http://searchcio.techtarget.com/definition/learning-management-system

Rubie-Davies, C. (2015). *Becoming a high expectation teacher: Raising the bar*. New York, NY: Routledge.

Sackstein, S. (2015). *Hacking assessment: 10 ways to go gradeless in a traditional grades school*. Cleveland, OH: Times 10.

Schaffhauser, D. (2014). Report: Most schools delivering BYOD programs, training teachers in mobile devices usage. *THE Journal*. Retrieved from https://thejournal.com/articles/2014/03/27/report-most-schools-delivering-byod-programs-training-teachers-in-mobile-devices-usage.aspx

Sheninger, E. C. (2016). *Uncommon learning: Creating schools that work for kids*. Thousand Oaks, CA: Corwin.

Sinek, S. (2009, Sept.). How great leaders inspire action (YouTube video). *TED^x* at Puget Sound. Retrieved from https://www.ted.com/talks/simon_sinek_how_great_leaders_inspire_action?language=en

Singer, N. (2015). Chromebooks gaining on Ipads in school sector. *Bits*. Retrieved from http://bits.blogs.nytimes.com/2015/08/19/chromebooks-gaining-on-ipads-in-school-sector/?_r=0

Staker, H. (2011, May). *The rise of K–12 blended learning: Profiles of emerging models*. Retrieved from http://www.christenseninstitute.org/publications/the -rise-of-k-12-blended-learning-profiles-of-emerging-models/

Strauss, V. (2013, October 16). Howard Gardner: "Multiple intelligences" are not "learning styles." *The Washington Post*. Retrieved from www.washingtonpost .com/news/answer-sheet/wp/2013/10/16/howard-gardner-multiple-intelligenc es-are-not-learning-styles

Summit Public Schools. (2015). *Explore a day in the life of a Summit student*. Retrieved from http://summitps.org/student-day?day=3

Taylor, H. (2015). Google's Chromebooks make up half of U.S. classroom devices sold. *CNBC*. Retrieved from www.cnbc.com/2015/12/03/googles-chromebooks -make-up-half-of-us-classroom-devices.html

Young, S. (2012, July). *The DIY degree: Using self-education to earn a bachelor's degree in 1 year*. Retrieved from https://www.scotthyoung.com/blog/2012/07/04/ the-diy-degree/

Index

A SAGE Publishing Company

Helping educators make the greatest impact

CORWIN HAS ONE MISSION: to enhance education through intentional professional learning.

We build long-term relationships with our authors, educators, clients, and associations who partner with us to develop and continuously improve the best evidence-based practices that establish and support lifelong learning.

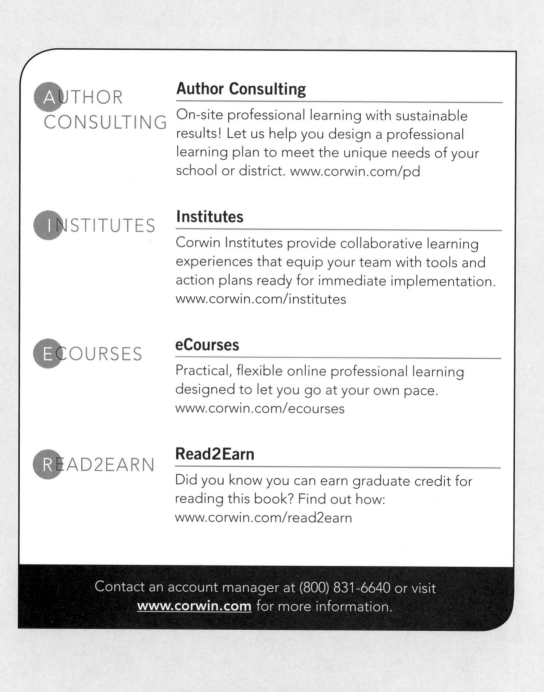